PRESENT AT THE REVOLUTION

by

Joanne L. Schweik
with Gordon Anderson

Gordon Anderson
Joanne L. Schweik

Published by Driftwood Press, P. O. Box A, Greenhurst, NY 14742.

1 3 5 7 9 10 8 6 4 2
First Edition ISBN 0-9748238-0-5
Published and printed in the United States of America

To my

lifetime partner,

my wife,

Geraldine

From Gordon

PRESENT AT THE REVOLUTION
(Biography of Gordon Anderson)

TABLE OF CONTENTS

PART ONE

PART TWO

PART THREE

INDEX

ACKNOWLEDGEMENTS

To writer, **Joanne Schweik**, who was willing to take complicated materials and issues and reduce them to understandable happenings. Thanks also for your advice, counsel and skill, Joanne.

To other contributors:

Donald L. Rexroad of Leisure Photography for the outstanding aerial photographs and others used throughout this book. See the Photo Credits page for reference to his many contributions. Thank you, Donald!

C. Frederick Falldine, my childhood friend and who, along with his wife, owns a Golf Pro Shop in West Palm Beach, Florida.

John Glenzer, a member of the Chautauqua County Legislature, later becoming the County Executive.

Christie Herbst, who was a reporter on the beat when I was a legislator. She is now the Editor of the Post Journal.

William Parment, a good friend who took over the sewer project after the legislature voted to have County Executive Joseph Gerace assume the task because he had a larger staff to handle the matter.

Eldon H. Johnson, whom I have known for 50+ years. He is Pastor Emeritus of Zion Covenant Church and encouraged me to write this book.

Rex Rotsko, our "surrogate" son, and the son of our engineer neighbor, John Rotsko. Rex repeatedly told me the "Driftwood Story" must be written up. Rex sorted reams and reams of papers in preparation for this book.

The late **R. Theodore Smith** who was formerly Dean at JCC and Chairman of the County Sewer Agency.

State Supreme Court Justice(retired), **Joseph Gerace** who urged me to record these memories for future generations.

Our two sons, **Daniel G. and David E. Anderson**. Daniel was invaluable as chief proofreader and critique. David prepared all of the pictures for this book requiring many hours of work.

Carl Brand who formatted this book and who displayed inordinate patience with us throughout all our many changes. I doubt anyone else would have been so kind.

A hearty thank you to all of you. This book could not have come into being without all of your help. If there are factual mistakes, I am sorry. We worked from county minutes, newspaper accounts and just plain memory on the part of several people. Finally, to all of those people who lent their leadership in years past, the late **Ernest D. Leet**, an attorney and catalyst of the sewer project and the late **John Luensman**, head of the Chautauqua County Planning Department for more than 30 years, and the late **Jess Present**, New York State Senator. If you feel your name should be in here, I am sorry we missed it. The book would never end!

As you will see, among those mentioned above, several important observers of the events chronicled here have written their own commentaries, which are in various sections of this book. I write all the "Significant Portraits" of people who have played key roles in my personal life

Gordon Anderson.

INTRODUCTION

As you read the pages of this book, you will discover some things you never knew and some things you may have forgotten about Gordon Anderson. He grew up much like other children of his time, but he possessed within himself a persistent, diligent and determined spirit. As he grew to manhood these qualities grew right along with him.

If there is a challenge to be faced, Gordon accepts that challenge and tries to make a situation better. This book will bring to light some of the challenges he encountered as he started out to face the world "on his own." It primarily focuses on eight years of exemplary perseverance as he served the people of the Towns of Ellery and Gerry in Chautauqua County as a legislator and, for two years, as the Chairman of that body. In spite of some very difficult circumstances, he counts it an honor to have served his turn in that capacity.

During Gordon's eight years in the legislature, there were some seemingly overwhelming obstacles which he took in stride, maintaining his "cool" throughout. He is the kind of person who remains calm but determined and, when all is said and done, he remains respected by his adversaries.

It has been my extreme joy to be married to this man for more than 47 years; his spirit of perseverance has pervaded our marriage and the rearing of our two sons. Life with Gordon has been adventurous and exciting, with many facets. Now we face together the sheer pleasure of yet another generation, our grandchildren, growing up before our very eyes. We are, indeed, blessed to be living near all of them.

Geraldine Anderson

PROLOGUE

Gordon Anderson, like many others in this area, is a second-generation Swede who began his journey in Jamestown, New York and, except for a ten-year hiatus in California, has lived through six decades in the Southwestern corner of New York State, with the Chautauqua Lake area as his focus. Probably that focus on – and love for – the lake has been central to his life. It has, in addition, spawned a commitment to activism that is the core of this book.

This story, though involving the entire life of one of our county's citizens, focuses mainly on some important things that happened in the years between 1964 and 1982 in Chautauqua County, New York: things that touched on the lives of many residents but might have touched them very differently if Gordon Anderson had not been where he was and had not done what he did here during those years.

Although his work life has been primarily in teaching, notably as a psychologist/social scientist at Jamestown Community College, Gordon's endeavors have branched out to the ministry, to business, and especially to politics. In 1971 he ran for, and was elected to, the first Chautauqua county legislature, where he served for eight years, the last two of them as chairperson of that body. Prior to his running for office, he led the effort to change the proposed route of Highway 17 (now U.S. Interstate Highway 86) in the Bemus Point area so it would save the homes on Driftwood Hill, including his own. Once in the County legislature, he was a leader in, and heavily involved in, "the revolution" of the 1970s, a term coined by now State Assemblyman William Parment to describe the monumental changes which Chautauqua County government launched to improve the lives of county citizens in the years from 1972 through the 1980s. That "revolution" included establishing the Office of the Aging, achieving a plan for recycling waste and establishing a central county solid waste landfill; coming to terms with and building a bridge over Chautauqua Lake so the "Southern Tier Expressway" (now I-86) could be completed; and, the most difficult and traumatic of all, sewering Chautauqua Lake to help eliminate the criminal pollution of the county's greatest asset.

Every human being who lives hopes to live a good life and have influence, one way or another. Gordon Anderson is certainly one who has contributed to the betterment of his personal connections, but more, to the citizens of his county through his many involvements. In fact, as this book proves, Gordon Anderson is truly one who has made a difference. What's more, this book tells a story that has not really been told before, and which everyone who cares about Chautauqua County should read.

PREFACE I

By Christie L. Herbst, editor, *Jamestown Post-Journal*

When Gordon E. Anderson announced he would not seek re-election to the Chautauqua County Legislature in the 1979 election, he described his eight years in office as "a citizen taking his turn in local government." This modest summation of the historic and sometimes tumultuous years he had served on the legislature is typical of his low-key style and an indication of his ultimate success in office: He never forgot why he was there.

In those years, the county legislature broke new trails, and with every step Gordie was there to set a style of leadership, both as minority leader and legislature chairman, that we have missed in the years since. Construction of the Chautauqua Lake South and Center Sewer Districts during his years in office remains today the most visible achievement. The subtlety of a photograph of Supreme Court Justice Joseph Gerace heartily congratulating Anderson when he was honored in mid-2003 by the county legislature is not lost on those who remember the firmness with which the two – Anderson, a Republican, and then-County Executive Gerace, a Democrat – had dealt with each other when they were in opposing leadership roles in the county some 25 years ago. The picture speaks well of both men.

Whether as leader of the loyal opposition of the legislature quoting George Orwell* to his colleagues, or as the chairman of the county's top governing body wrestling with the knotty and emotionally charged problems of developing a lake management district, Gordie was always doing what he thought best for his constituents and his county. He was in those years and is today a gentleman and, we who know him add with affection, a stubborn Swede who simply is not deterred by adversity.

Gordie was right in the middle of it in the key years when county government did the single best thing it has ever done for Chautauqua Lake – creating the sewer districts. To say it wasn't easy is an understatement and the account of what happened shouldn't be lost in local history. With his honesty and intuitiveness, Gordie Anderson is the best one to tell the story.

* The quote was "All animals are equal, but some animals are more equal than others." It was the famous satiric observation from George Orwell's *Animal Farm* (1945, chapter 10).

PREFACE II

By William L. Parment, Member, New York State Assembly

During the 1970s Chautauqua County government exploded. The match that lit the fuse for this explosion was the U.S. Supreme Court decision, Baker vs. Carr (1964). The decision resulted in the court imposing the requirement of one-person-one-vote on all legislative bodies and led to a revolution in the structure and the activity of Chautauqua County government. Subsequent to that ruling, Busti town supervisor Joseph Gerace and Dr. Glen Ebersole brought suit in Federal District Court against the County Board of Supervisors challenging the composition of that board as being malapportioned and not in compliance with the tenets of Baker vs. Carr.

To give an idea of the degree of malapportionment, the Town of Arkwright had a 1970 population of 826 people and they had one town supervisor and one vote on the old county board. The Town of Pomfret, which had a population of approximately 10,000 people, also had one supervisor and one vote on that old board.

The Federal District Court ruled in favor of the Gerace-Ebersole suit and ordered the Board of Supervisors to restructure itself to comply with the one-person-one-vote principle. This ruling led to a revolution in Chautauqua County government. Under court supervision the board, in 1971, created a 25-member legislative body based on some single-member and some multi-member districts of proportionately equal population. This 25-member plan was drawn by the Republican Party because the Democrats were still very much in the minority on the County Board of Supervisors.

The first election held under the new plan in 1971 resulted in the election of 15 Democrats and 10 Republicans, a dramatic reversal. Although the Democrats won control of county government for the first time ever, there were also a number of new Republican members elected, and one of them was Gordon Anderson from the Town of Ellery. After the 1971 election, when the county moved from the malapportioned old Board of Supervisors to a population-based legislative scheme of 25 members, the needs and desires of the people of Chautauqua County began to be addressed by the county government, with Gordon Anderson playing a very active role in that process.

The Legislature began by establishing a commission charged with creating a new county charter which, when it was completed, would mandate an elected county executive. It was the political judgment of the people involved that previous attempts to create a charter had failed because they had followed the county-manager form. It was strongly felt that the public wanted an executive who was elected. The new charter was approved by the legislature and by a vote of the people of Chautauqua County. The county also went through redistricting subsequent to the 1971 court-imposed plan and settled on a 25-member County Legislature with single-member districts of substantially equal population.

During this period the county had signed an agreement with the City of Jamestown to assume management of the Chautauqua County Airport. The legislature also created the Chautauqua County Industrial Development Agency and started the first Office for the Aging in New York State. They expanded the County Health Department and its concern for mental health, and by the end of the '70s decade, included extensive services for the disabled citizens of the county. They responded to a real need for convenient placement of county offices and moved the Motor Vehicle Department offices to Jamestown and Dunkirk.

The County, through the legislature, took over solid waste management from the towns and the two cities (Dunkirk and Jamestown), and built the first landfill in the state that was compliant with both the National Environmental Policy Act and the State Environmental Quality Review Act. Other innovations included taking over some streets from the two cities, something that is still not done anywhere else in New York State; building two industrial parks; merging the county and city of Jamestown social services districts; and beginning the process of merging some of the smaller police agencies into the County Sheriff's Department.

In addition, the county, through aggressive sewer and water district boards, also embarked on an effort to create sewer and water districts. The legislature designated the South and Center Chautauqua Lake Sewer Districts and the North Chautauqua Lake Sewer District, which allowed the county to avail itself of monies appropriated under Federal Law 92-500, the so-called "Clean Water Act," which was sponsored in the U.S. Senate by Edward Muskie. Through that act the county was able to obtain significant federal funding for the creation of these sewer districts around Chautauqua Lake, as well as in villages such as Brocton, Sherman, Silver Creek and the hamlet of Ripley.

Progress went smoothly in the North Chautauqua Lake Sewer District. The South and Center districts, however, had significant problems due to a critical error in the engineering phase when the design engineer failed to do a plasticity test on the soil at the location of the treatment plant. This failure caused the engineer to overestimate the resistance of the soil and to make errors in the design of the piling necessary to create a foundation for the treatment plant. The original design called for friction piles but had to be changed to end-bearing piles after the construction was underway. This change resulted in substantial cost over-runs in the construction of the plant. The same error resulted in difficulties in the construction of the gravity-flow sewers. This type of sewer requires that you go deeper and deeper into the ground as the line runs laterally, with the flow to the pump station going as deep as 40 feet below the surface. You then pump the effluent back to the surface and allow gravity to take it to the next pump station. When the contractor started to get down to the required depth at the pump stations, the soil was so plastic that it collapsed the walls of the excavation. The sheet piles collapsed and the work had to be halted. These problems resulted in project cost escalating from $18 to $32 million.

The sewer board was monitoring this and knew that there would be additional unavoidable costs. When it came to the point where they had consumed $18 million, they expected to authorize an additional amount of money to complete the project. The sewer board assumed they could do this on their own authority by simply increasing the authorization for bonding. The New York state legislature, however, had recently passed legislation requiring a permissive referendum on any increases. By this time, the public was so upset with the project that they wouldn't vote for increases. Eventually the sewer district ran out of money, the contractor stopped work, and the sewer board turned to the county legislature for help. The legislature, of which Gordon Anderson was then the chairman, voted to dissolve the sewer board and take control of the project. They transferred power to the County Executive, Joseph Gerace. The project was subsequently brought to a successful completion.

This was all going on at the same time that the county was closing all of the municipal dumps in the county and trying to open a central landfill, causing controversy that included cost, town identity and location. Because the county chose the town of Ellery for the new central landfill, Gordon Anderson was confronted with another problem in his own backyard. Anderson had, by this time, risen to the post of chairman of the county legislature and thus had to deal with the projects not only as leader of the legislature but as a locally elected official in the district most affected. Between cost over-runs, environmental protests, town resentment of the county, and the not-in-my-backyard objections by Town of Ellery residents, Gordon Anderson had his hands full. On the one hand, he was elected from Ellery – to represent that district – and on the other hand, he was chairman of the county legislature and he was trying to balance two responsibilities.

It was a period of great controversy, as is often the case in a period of great change. This was basically a period of revolution in county government. There were an amazing number of new programs started and completed and changes were made to the basic structure of county government.

Other activities that took place during this time included the construction of the Southern Tier Expressway and the bridge across Chautauqua Lake. A major portion of this work was again in Gordon Anderson's legislative district. The bridge across the lake was especially controversial. A lawsuit stopped construction for five years and local officials had to lobby extensively to restart the process.

Gordon Anderson was also involved in the construction of a new Agricultural Center for Chautauqua County that brought together in one place the Cornell Cooperative Extension Service and the local offices of the Federal Department of Agriculture. This project, although not nearly as controversial as the sewer project, the landfill or the lake bridge, did involve a considerable exchange of ideas and some consternation.

And so, when you look back on the 1970s in Chautauqua County, you find great change and great progress. You find a time of complexity, controversy, and concerned leadership. It was a time of government revolution that set the stage for the progress that Chautauqua County continues to enjoy today. Gordon Anderson not only played a major part in this drama, but he helped change the very stage on which future leaders in Chautauqua County play their roles.

(NOTE: William L. Parment was employed by Chautauqua County from July of 1970 to December of 1982, first as a planner and later as director of public works. He had a first-hand view of government operations during the entire 1970s.)

PREFACE III

By John A. Glenzer
Former County Executive and Legislator

It has been more than twenty years since I served on the Chautauqua County Legislature with Gordon Anderson. Unlike fine wine, memory does not improve with age. My comments will, therefore, lack specific examples, but will reflect a lasting impression of Gordon.

When Gordon took over the general oversight of the Chautauqua Lake South and Center Sewer Districts when he became legislature chairman in 1978, it was a mess in many ways. Cost overruns were the rule, rather than the exception. One legislator contended that the whole project was tainted by a series of scandals. None of this person's allegations were ever proved but they tended to generate confrontations between the citizens of the sewer districts and both the sewer district management and the Chautauqua County government.

My memories of the several meetings the legislature conducted with the citizens of the district are far from pleasant. Rumors that usually inflated the proposed costs to residents had the affluent mad and most of the elderly afraid that they could lose their homes. The lunatic fringe that usually surfaces in the middle of any stressful situation was well-represented in the sewer district debates. Civility was often the least demonstrated social skill. Gordon Anderson was thrust into a leadership role as County Legislature Chairman. Then the engineers for the sewer project encountered quicksand in the project area and had to regroup to deal with it. Many times Gordie must have felt that he had stepped into that same quicksand.

Individuals don't inherit leadership positions in the Chautauqua County Legislature; like Smith Barney they "earn them." For most of us leadership qualities are easier to recognize than to define. Gordie not only acted like a leader, he dressed like one. When I recall Gordie, I see him with a suit and tie and shirt – none of which ever seemed to wrinkle.

Gordon gave, and inspired, loyalty. Maintaining the integrity of the party caucus was important. I don't recall any of us bolting once we had agreed as to how we would vote. We had an agreement that if, during the debate, we changed our mind we would call a meeting of the caucus to discuss what new information had caused any of us to recon-sider our vote. To fail to do so would have been a betrayal and we all respected Gordie too much to betray him.

The word contentious is often too mild a term to describe the debate on the floor of the legislature. Gordie was able to overcome much of this because he tended to attack problems and not people. His example led to a much more civilized level of behavior on the legislature floor than is often demonstrated.

Gordon Anderson served on the legislature because he wanted to serve the people of Chautauqua County. This, not ego, was his purpose and one of the main reasons he was such a valuable member of the legislature.

Gordon inherited a terrible situation when he assumed the role of guiding the sewer projects. He was unselfish in giving his time, energy and talents to helping the residents of the several communities that make up the South and Center Sewer Districts. Through his efforts what appeared to be an unmanageable situation was converted to a situation with a light at the end of the tunnel. When Bill Parment, then Director of the Chautauqua County Department of Public Works, took over the project, it was under control and well on the way to completion.

Bill Parment demonstrated the same determination to successful completion of this project that Gordon had shown. Both men deserve the thanks of the sewer district residents for a job well done.

PART 1

THE MAKING
OF A CITIZEN

CHAPTER ONE

I WAS BORN AT THE USUAL AGE

Gordon Anderson was born on August 3, 1932—a depression baby. "When I was born, everyone was depressed," he says.

His father, Edwin, was unemployed that year, in spite of a promise from the owner of Crescent Tool, where he worked, that all workers would be kept on. Karl Peterson, the owner, was not able to keep his promise in the economy of the Great Depression. So Edwin, who kept a journal of his yearly earnings, recorded that he earned only $300 in the year of his son's birth, and he kept himself busy by making gravel with a large ball-peen hammer in his driveway from stone gathered in the undeveloped neighborhood. He worked briefly at Blackstone Corporation, through the efforts of Norris Foote, and helped his brother-in-law rebuild his car engine.

1) Franz Elmgren 1860-1925

As Gordon puts it, "I am made with Swedish parts, but I was assembled in Jamestown." This is a reference to his grandparents, all of whom were born in Sweden, and four of whom later individually emigrated to the United States, two to the Jamestown area and two to the Collinsburg, PA area just below Pittsburgh, and then on to Jamestown.

One great-grandfather was Franz Elmgren[1], who was the first paid speaker and organizer for the Social Democratic party in Sweden in the 19th century. He traveled widely throughout the country, speaking and "agitating" support for changing the heavily class-oriented society and big landowners to Socialist Democratic principles. He wrote a book, *30 år som agitator*, and many years later a novel was written about him, *Musikanternas Uttåg*, by P. O. Enquist. There is a large monument to Elmgren in Jönköping, Sweden, commemorating his work. In recent years a street, Elmgrensgatan[2], was named in honor of him in the same city. However, to his family—or, rather, families, for it is known he had two and may have had three different ones with three different women—he is not such a hero. Gordon Anderson's

2) Gordon F.E. Elmgrensgatan

grandmother Hilfred, for instance, wanted nothing to do with him or his fame, and neither did Anna, Hilfred's sister. When Anna was a young woman, Franz offered her a college education—he had softened some by then—but she turned it down. Still, it may be that some of Gordon's bent for organizing and for politics is a legacy from this great-grandfather.

In light of this history about his great-grandfather Elmgren, Gordon was shocked to find in the Elmgren autobiography a real irony: that Franz Elmgren and P. P. Wallenström had been political and religious combatants. Wallenström[3] started the Mission Covenant Church in Sweden, which Gordon then became a member of after the church had established roots in the United States. Thereby Gordon felt a connection to Wallenström. The Swedish founder was a brilliant man but somewhat brash, who had earned his Ph.D. at Uppsala University, not in Swedish but in Latin! The struggle between him and Elmgren began when the "agitator" was speaking at a labor rally on the island of Gotland. At some point Wallenström interrupted him and tried to take over the podium to present the Gospel of Christ, and also interfered in this way on another occasion. In Gordon's words, "I think they were competitors for the minds and hearts of their listeners. I just think it was a real irony that my church and my great-grandfather were involved with each other all those years ago." An interesting footnote to this story is that the Mission Covenant Church became a powerful force in Sweden, eventually becoming second only to the Social Democrats in members elected to Parliament.

Gordon's other Swedish ancestors were all hardworking citizens[4] with peasant-stock backgrounds, most of them very poor. When they arrived in America, however, like other Swedish immigrants who fled poverty and starvation in their homeland for the promise offered by the American dream, they managed to improve their status. So Gordon relates that when his parents, Edwin Anderson and Ebba Brostrom, who were first generation Swedish-Americans, married in 1931, they were able to fill their newly built house with new furnishings for which they paid cash. Most people couldn't do that today.

When Gordon was about two years old, his mother was able to get a short stint of temporary employment at Crescent Tool, and Gordon was left in the care of his father[5] and his Aunt, Elsie Ulander. "And," says Gordon, "I was not happy about my mother being away."

His parents were both devout Christians. His father had promised his mother that he would take their little boy to Sunday School when he was two. Thus was begun an important thread in the young boy's life—toward a lifetime of commitment to Christ, including the ministry, which was to become, in addition to teaching and politics, a significant area of leadership and service.

THE COTTAGE AT CONNELLY PARK

rom his youngest days, Gordon experienced[6] summer life on the lake as idyllic and wonderful. His father and grandfather had helped get themselves through the Great Depression by muskie fishing in the lake and selling the fish in the public market in Jamestown's Brooklyn Square[7], Gordon recalls:

6) Gordon and his friend Bear

"We had no electricity, no running water. (Later it became my job to hike to the spring and bring pure water back in pails for our household needs. That is one of my most vivid memories.) In Jamestown things were delivered to our home—fish, ice, milk. At the lake, things were more primitive. We had a 'chunk' stove in the living room for heat and a kerosene lamp for light. The cottage had its own unique, pleasant smell.

"A typical meal was fish, boiled potatoes, sill, applesauce, peaches or pears and, sometimes biscuits and 'medvurst.' Grandma picked berries when in season as a special treat. We had a kerosene stove for baking. We also had a chemical toilet.

"When Grandpa died, Grandma gave the cottage to my dad, who put in electricity. He and Victor Olson (my grandmother's uncle) drilled a well, but the water tasted and smelled of sulfur. We still used the spring for drinking water."

When Gordon was in high school, his father gave him a boat of his own—which he named "Sweetie Pie[8]," and he used it well, especially for recreation and attracting the girls he dated. Sweetie Pie ultimately became the courting boat for Gordon and Geri, his wife-to-be.

Gordon again: "There were lots of kids now—two Falldines, two Johnsons. Victor had sold his cottage to the Hunts who also had two children, Dick and Pat[9], and later the Folletts had two also. My cousin Carolyn Larson[10], who was four years old when her mother died, was like a sister to me (I was seven). We slept together in my parents' room at the cottage on a trundle bed. Her brother Howard[11], who was ten years older, would row us up to the huge lily pads near Hadley's Bay in front of the Stow property, where we caught large sunfish, bluegills, calico bass, perch, etc.

"Carolyn's father had a house near us in Jamestown so we played Monopoly during the winter months. To this day she hates Monopoly and never plays it because I always beat her. I don't play it either since I had a record of winning and don't want to spoil it. We also put up my electric train and played with that."

SCHOOL DAYS

ordon went to school in Jamestown—starting early in kindergarten, the first year Fletcher school[12] was opened, in 1937, though he could have been held back a year because he had just turned five. He was in the first class that went through Fletcher from K-6.

By the time he was nine he was studying the violin[13,13A], thus beginning another lifelong interest. He found his father's neglected violin in the attic, and asked to be allowed to take lessons. His parents declined, saying he was too young.

"But me being me," Gordon says, characterizing his usual persistence, "I called a violin teacher I knew about and asked him to contact my parents to ask them to allow me to take lessons. He did, and my parents agreed." In due time, Gordon became a resource for his elementary music teacher. He played for staged square dancing at Fletcher School, with the teacher sending a taxi for his transport to play for square dancing in other elementary schools.

"I had a blue satin coat with tails that I wore when I played at staged square dances," Gordon relates.

However, being small for his age (as he was until he finally reached maturity in his first year of college), he began his studies on a 3/4-size instrument. By the time he was in his late high school years, he had his own radio show, which he called "Magic Melodies," where he played the violin with piano accompaniment.

13) Playing his violin

In high school he was concertmaster[14,14a] of the orchestra for two years, and won an Arion award for music. He also sang in the A Cappella choir, directed by Ebba Goranson[15], with whom he had a special relationship. Her father, a church musician in Chicago, accepted a call to the Swedish Mission Church. His name was N. R. Goranson. He came with his wife and two adult children, Ebba and Arthur. Gordon relates, "One day Ebba bawled me out for something I did, or didn't, do. Afterwards, she took me to Lindy's for a hamburger. That was 'Aunt Ebba.'"

During this time, Gordon says, "I was asked by Marvin Heldeman, a high school classmate, to play violin at his YWCA concert. He played the piano, and though he had polio in one arm, he was an excellent pianist. While he rested, I came out as the featured violinist, with Ruth Moe at the piano. I couldn't remember the first note, even though I had practiced a hundred times. I had to go get my music. Thereafter I was a little nervous not to have music or lecture notes.

"It was a big thrill for me, when I was 16, that my Mom and Dad took me to hear concert violinist Isaac Stern play at a packed auditorium of 3000 people at Jamestown High School. I got his autograph and to this day I still have it."

Through these years, during the school year, he lived with his parents on Cole Avenue in Jamestown. In many activities, often with his cousin Carolyn, he pursued a normal childhood-adolescent life, as it would have been lived in the 1940s in small communities in America. For Gordon this normalcy was embellished by his natural bent toward curiosity, persistence, wit and humor, and sometimes carelessness. For instance, on Cole Avenue he built a chemistry lab in the basement and accidentally put a nail through a thermostat wire, thus causing a heating crisis in the house. When his parents finally figured out the cause of their problem, they weren't angry, Gordon says; they just teased him about it for years.

Another outlet for his early exercise of leadership and enterprise was in his religious commitment. By his own testimony he "accepted Jesus Christ as my Savior" at the age of 12 at a crusade led by Jack Wyrtsen, who was a well-known evangelist for Word of Life Ministries. Soon after that he met Jimmie Davis, whose influence was of great importance in Gordon's developing spiritual life. That life would always include a ministry component, eventually resulting in ordination as a minister and stints as pastor or temporary pastor of a number of churches.

When he graduated from Jamestown High School in 1950 (at age 17), Gordon was well on the way to a career marked by leadership in a number of fields — religion, teaching, politics, business, and, not to be left out, exemplary citizenship ("except," he jokes, "when I gave two teachers exploding fountain pens on April Fool's Day!")

CONNELLY PARK, ANOTHER VIEW
By C. Frederick Falldine

I don't remember ever not knowing the joys of summers at Connelly Park[16]. When I search my memory for the earliest recollections of my life, I recall a scene, not so joyful, in back of our cottage at Connelly Park. I was probably two or three years old, Mom and Dad were getting into their car to leave on a trip of some kind (I still don't know what or where or for how long) and I was crying—screaming, really—I guess because I thought I was being abandoned forever. Actually my grandparents were there to take care of Jan, my older sister, and me, so all was under control. Not a significant event in itself, perhaps, but it's the beginning of my memories and it happened at Connelly Park.

16) Gordie, Freddie, Bob Folette and a friend

I also don't remember ever not knowing Gordie Anderson. He is Dr. Gordon E. Anderson now; then he was Gordie, and to me he will always be Gordie. To my grandfather he was "Stubs," a nickname Grandpa gave Gordie when he was little and one Grandpa continued to use even as Gordie grew older. Gordie was my best friend at Connelly Park, which made him my first best friend. Although he was three years older than me, it didn't affect our ability to relate and to enjoy the same things.

As best I can recall, the Connellys owned a dairy farm on a hill about thirteen miles north of Jamestown on the west side of Chautauqua Lake. Before my time—probably in the early 1900s—they built a road east from the highway fronting the farm down the hill to the lake, and extended the road both north and south, parallel to the shore, creating a number of lots which they sold and upon which were built cottages of wide-ranging shapes and sizes. This subdivision became known as Connelly Park.

The last six lots at the end of the south fork, somewhat remote from the rest of the subdivision, formed a separate little community. The cottages were very similar in construction and had probably been built at about the same time. In my time there, they were owned by, from north to south, the Folletts, the Johnsons, the Falldines, the John Andersons[17], the Hunts and the Edwin Andersons (no relation to John). When I think of Connelly Park, it is really this small community that I think of, and it is there that I spent summers from before that very first recollection until I was fourteen years old.

Jan and I had a great group of playmates. Joann and Roger Johnson, next door to us to the north, were from New York City; Patty and Dick Hunt, two doors to the south, were from Corry, PA; and Gordie, in the last cottage to the south, was from Jamestown. We were all close friends and we swam and played games together.

In the early years, living in the cottage was only a step or two above camping out. We had no electricity and no indoor plumbing. Our lights were kerosene lamps and our heat, if we needed any, was a kerosene space heater in the living room. Water came from a pump in the backyard. There was a toilet in a small bathroom on the back porch, which was flushed by pouring a bucket of water

18) Connelly Park Spring

into the toilet bowl. It was the user's responsibility to re-fill that bucket from the pump after each flush; woe unto him who failed to fulfill that requirement.

Food was kept refrigerated in an old-fashioned icebox. The iceman brought big blocks of ice periodically, often enough to keep food from spoiling. It was not unusual to see a box of crabs on the block of ice. Live crabs were used for bait, both for bass and for bullheads, and they had to be kept fresh, too. Mom seemed to tolerate that just fine.

The pump water was drinkable but tasted of sulfur. A better alternative was to bring water from a spring[18] about a quarter of a mile down the road. Gordie and I were too small to carry a full bucket of water that far, so we rigged a sturdy pole with a small notch in the middle for the bucket handle. With one of us at each end of the pole, we could carry full buckets from the spring. Thus we became the bucket brigade, and most of the time there was fresh cold spring water in the icebox for drinking and cooking.

I don't remember that any of us, adults or children, ever complained that these living conditions were too primitive; on the contrary, it really was like camping out and we all enjoyed it as such.

Spring and early summers were berry-picking time. The hills above and behind the cottages were full of wild strawberries. We could go to the field and in one small area pick a pail full of sweet, delicious strawberries in no time (filling ourselves as we filled the pails). The result was some wonderful shortcakes and ice cream sundaes.

The hillside across the dirt road from the cottages had many elderberry bushes. One weekend each spring the families would join in an "elderberry fest." The men and boys would fill bushel baskets with the berries, then strip the berries from the stems into pans. The women would wash the berries and make jam and jelly with some, then can the rest to use for pies the rest of the year. At the end of the day, the reward would be fresh hot elderberry pie a la mode for all. I can still taste it!

In time, electricity, running water and indoor plumbing came to Connelly Park. I'm sure the adults appreciated the improvements more than we kids did, although I do remember thinking, when I took my first shower in our new bathroom, that it was more pleasant than a weekly trip into the lake with a bar of soap, which had previously constituted my bath.

As to our activities, we whiled away the summers swimming, boating, picnicking, playing croquet and badminton, reading and a fair amount of just plain goofing off. But without a doubt, the most serious pursuit for Gordie and me was fishing; in all the time we were together at Connelly Park, we spent literally hundreds of hours fishing. Sometimes we'd dig up worms for bait and drop lines near weeds or lily pads and catch a meal or two worth of "punkinseeds," which was our catchall name for small pan fish (sunfish, bluegills, rock bass, etc.). We would clean them to get them ready for frying, and even though they had a lot of small bones, they made a tasty meal.

Our more serious fishing was for muskellunge—muskie, for short. Each spring we would each buy a muskie license, which came with five tags, one of which had to be clamped through the mouth and gills of each "keeper." (A muskie had to be at least 32 inches long to keep; if it was shorter it had to be released.) The tags were not reusable, so each fisherman was limited to five keepers per year. Gordie and I would take one of our motorboats out to troll for muskies using hand lines with either spoons or plugs as lures. In all the years we fished together, logging many hours, we only landed three or four keepers. Looking back on that, maybe it should have seemed like a waste of time, but I only remember it as enjoyable time well spent.

We did some live-bait fishing also, which meant we first had to catch some minnows. We would set bait traps in minnow streams back in the hills above the lake, wait a day or two and retrieve the traps. We'd select the largest minnows and put them into a bait pail, which we would then keep in the stream below the spring where we got our drinking water. When it was fishing time, we would go to the spring and bring back the bait pail, which we tied to the side of the boat, letting it float partly submerged so the minnows

19) The first CARTS buses

would stay alive. We'd each use a fly rod and put a minnow on each hook, then row the boat slowly through waters that we hoped would yield bass or maybe even a muskie, letting the minnow bait swim as normally as possible to look tempting. We never caught a muskie this way but we did land some nice bass.

Gordie was very creative and a good teacher. In town we built "jitneys[19]" (our version of soapbox racers) constructed from orange crates, four-by-fours, wheels on axles, rope and a steering wheel. He had built them before I was old enough to be involved; he taught me how and we built several together. At the lake, we would carve small boats from wood blocks, attach them to the lines of our fishing poles and have boat races.

At Connelly Park our families each had a small boat with a five-horsepower motor, which we used for fishing, trips to the store in Stow or just riding around on the lake. Gordie taught me how to take the motor apart, clean it and put it back together. We would service both motors regularly, and they almost always worked smoothly and dependably.

In addition to being inventive, Gordie was also very mischievous, and I was a very willing accomplice. We were always trying to devise ways to play tricks on the other kids. One such event took place when Gordie stayed over one night. The upstairs of our cottage was one large room divided by curtains to form two separate "bedrooms" for Jan and me[20]. That afternoon Gordie and I tied a string to a roller skate, and another string to a bunch of coat hangers, the idea being, after we were all in bed with the lights out, to pull the skate from Jan's side to ours and to rattle the coat hangers, hoping to give her a good scare. We first pulled the coat hanger string, which scared her. Then the plan went awry when the string to the skate caught on a clothesbasket on Jan's side, which of course we couldn't see, and when Gordie pulled the string, the clothesbasket fell over with a loud crash. I think it scared Gordie and me even more than it did Jan.

Then there was the time we used flour to turn our black cat, "Blackie," into a pretty realistic skunk look-alike. We were able to coax him to meander into a coffee klatch gathering of neighborhood ladies; he really created a stir, much to our delight.

On one of our earliest fishing outings together, when I was quite small, Gordie got the boat to where we would start fishing. When he started to my end of the boat to drop the anchor, I insisted I was big enough to handle it. As Gordie tells it, I somehow managed to get the anchor over the side but I went in with it. He still laughs when he describes me sitting on the bottom of the lake with the anchor in my lap and bubbles rising to the surface along with my glasses.

There was, of course, a serious side to Gordie as well. He was raised in what I consider a strong Christian environment. His family lived their faith in a way that, while not intrusively overt, made it clear to those of us around them that they were very confident in the teachings of the Bible. I've always believed that my friendship with Gordie during the Connelly Park years played a significant part in my development into a responsible, ethical, Christian adult.

Summers at Connelly Park were idyllic in the truest sense of that word. Of course, I didn't appreciate at the time how great a time it was. To be sure, I looked forward to summer at the lake but it has taken the passing of time and the experiences of adulthood to make me more fully appreciate how carefree and peaceful those summers were.

(*Note: Freddie Falldine's grandfather was, along with Karl Peterson, a major stockholder of Crescent Tool Co. in Jamestown.)

SIGNIFICANT PORTRAITS

GRANDFATHER—LUDWIG ANDERSON

My grandfather, Ludwig (Louie) Anderson[21], was raised on a dairy farm called Ryggåsen[22], near Vimmerby, Sweden. The terrain is somewhat similar to the moon in that it is filled with rocks, which the cows had to graze around. The farm was located on a lake called Yxern. Peter Andersson[23], my great-grandfather, and his three boys fished through the ice in winter since there wasn't quite as much farm work to be done then. They would load the fish on a wagon or sleigh and sell them in Vimmerby. Often they would all get drunk, using the money they got for the fish to buy liquor. This had a bad effect on my Grandpa because he ultimately

21) Ludwig Anderson

became an alcoholic. He was, as it is called, an epsilon drinker. He would be sober for long periods of time and then would drink, sometimes for weeks, but always at home. He became very mean when he was drunk, frightening both my dad and my grandmother.

My Grandpa Anderson emigrated to the United States in 1902 at the age of 23. He worked in Ludlow, PA at the tanning factory to pay for his passage; he then came to Jamestown where he met Hilfred and eventually married her at the home of Victor and Freida Olson on Lake Street in Jamestown.

Grandpa gravitated towards Lake Chautauqua, which perhaps reminded him of Yxern. He bought a shed off of a barge[24] and slipped it on Connelly's land very near a superb spring. Later, Grandpa rolled the shanty[25] on discarded telephone poles to the lot he and Victor Olson bought together. The land was very low and, by hand, Grandpa and my dad, who was 16, and sometimes Vic Olson[26], dug shale and clay out of the bank with a pickax and, using a wooden wheelbarrow, filled the lot in. It was like Ryggåsen: the lake, fishing, and cows grazing on the other side of the fence that went right into the lake[27]. The lot was the last in the Connelly allotment. Grandpa mockingly called his shanty "Le Hotel" and he would carry his fishing poles back and forth on the trolley from Jamestown[28], the line of which was halfway up the hill from the shanty. I'll bet the railway men loved that!

Grandpa Louie and Vic Olson hired someone to build two identical small cottages costing $700 each. I have the receipt[28A] dated June 22, 1925. When Grandpa bought the land, he made sure a right to the spring was in the deed even though it was 800 feet away. The cottage was primitive, no electricity, no running water, a chemical toilet and a wood-burning stove. The "refrigerator" was a hole dug in the bank with a kind of door, similar to what they had in Scandinavia. Because the earth cellar was not sanitary, we eventually got an icebox. When we needed ice, a drive to Stow was required. The square-shaped building in Stow[29], which had been part of the Chautauqua Traction Company, became an icehouse where ice harvested from the lake was stored. Although my grandpa didn't drive, he bought a 1928 Buick with the understanding that my dad would take him where he needed to go. In the heat of the summer, any ice we bought was half melted by the time we got it back to Connelly Park from Stow, as we carried it on the front bumper.

Grandpa gave me a desk when I was two and a half, which had been made at Monitor Furniture, where he worked. My parents felt that was foolish, but it turned out to be timely. My grandpa died when I was just three and a half years old. I remember a little bit about him.

My dad took over the cottage so I have a deep feeling about the lake. That is where I stayed every summer. It was a wonderful childhood in a Swedish tradition with my mom, my dad and my grandma.

G.A.

SIGNIFICANT PORTRAITS

GRANDMOTHER—HILFRED ANDERSON

M y grandmother, Hilfred Anderson[31,32] lived with us for many years. She had a very sad life. Her father, F. E. Elmgren, abandoned her and his pregnant wife in Sweden when my grandmother was a young girl. Her mother remarried, to a man whose name was Jonsson. Sadly, her apron caught fire one day as she was making jelly and she burned to death at the age of 46. Hilfred emigrated to the United States at age 18, sponsored by her uncle, Victor Olson, who owned a meat market at Barrett and Newland Avenues in Jamestown. She met and married Ludwig Anderson[33], who came to Jamestown after his passage agreement was fulfilled at a tanning factory in Ludlow, PA.

31) Hilfred Elmgren Anderson

They had one son, my dad Edwin[34]. She became a widow at age 56, during the great depression. My parents took over her home and my father agreed to take care of her. She got along very well with my parents, since all three of them were devoted Christians.

Grandmother Hilfred had no earning skills, but she did a lot of quilting, crocheting and embroidery. She embroidered a picture[35] for me when I was eight or nine years old. She made many quilts for the cottage. She had a broken ankle, which hadn't healed very well and caused her to limp. My dad teasingly called her "Limpy." But she was quiet and loving and never complained except if she had done handiwork for money and then people didn't pay her.

Her devotion to Christ and her church, First Lutheran, was deep, even though she didn't remember when she had accepted Christ. In 1947, she suffered a very bad stroke and was then confined to her bed for six and a half years. People who came to cheer her up left cheered up themselves. She told me that since she couldn't do anything else, she prayed a lot for me. My mother lovingly cared for her. She was the best grandma anyone could have, and I have many loving memories of her.

G.A.

SIGNIFICANT PORTRAITS

FATHER—EDWIN W. ANDERSON

 y dad, Edwin[36], was only 16 when my Grandpa acquired the land at Connelly Park. He was a gentle and wonderful man in spite of the fact that his father, my Grandpa Louie was not a very good role model. He made up his mind to behave differently because he loathed his father's behavior when he was drunk. Dad was a hard worker, had high energy, loved to fish[37,37A] and loved the lake, and he was a generous man. Part of his desire for different behavior was related to his conversion at an evangelistic meeting held by Rev. Gustav F. Johnson at Zion Mission Covenant Church in Jamestown around 1935. Dad became a zealous Christian and learned the Word of God. (He had been a nominal Lutheran.) He was elected to the Deacon Board at Zion Church and in due time became a Sunday School teacher.

36) My Dad Edwin Anderson, 70 years old

During the Depression, Dad worked a short time at Blackstone Corp. After that he went back to Crescent Tool and in 1938, because of a strike at Crescent Tool, he took a job at J. B. Williams Tool Co. in Buffalo where he made $100 a week! But eventually he came back to Crescent Tool. He was lonely for my mom and me. I have the letters he wrote to us while he was away.

Prior to World War II, Dad spent a lot of time with us. He took Grandma Anderson, my mom and me to the 1939 World's Fair[38]. I remember him saying to me as the ferry approached the Manhattan skyline, "I know you are a young boy, but try to remember what you see." It helped!

Most of the time on that trip I stayed in East Orange, NJ, with "Aunt Jenny," who was Victor Olson's sister; I was "too small" to go to the fair, except the one time.

That same year, Mom and Dad bought me a 1939 Lionel Electric train for Christmas. This was the first year these trains were made with a whistle. Later, Dad bought gates for the tracks and mounted it on paneling so it was easier to put up and take down. I still have it and, when it was 50 years old, we had a big party with shrimp, cake and good friends. The running train blew its whistle in appreciation.

Now World War II was upon us. Dad was continually deferred because of his skill as a die and toolmaker at Crescent Tool in Jamestown[39]. Because he had quit school at age 16, he earned his G.E.D. diploma and was promoted to foreman of the die department[40] with about 35 men under his charge. Crescent Tool also enrolled him in several correspondence courses from LaSalle University dealing with several subjects, one being personnel management. Dad was credited with developing two impressions instead of one on a die block, which almost doubled production. He retired from Crescent Tool Co. after nearly 50 years of employment there.

In the springtime, while I was growing up, Dad and I fished for bullheads using shrimp, which we purchased at the City Market in Jamestown, for bait. Nowadays, we eat the shrimp. Nuts to the bullheads!

As soon as school was out, we moved to the cottage. Every evening after dinner we would go fishing together, either casting or trolling for muskies or bass. Sometimes we used soft-shelled crabs for bait. On one occasion, Dad caught a 33-pound muskie while he was night fishing alone in his double-pointed Adirondack rowboat, which is similar to a canoe. "Cornstalk" weeds were a problem in Hadley's Bay, but that is where the fish were. We learned to cast over the weeds.

In 1956, Dad sold the cottage and the Cole Avenue house in Jamestown because he thought I would never return from California, and he wanted only one house to take care of. The newly purchased home was on Driftwood Road. It had lake rights so he could still enjoy fishing. When we moved back from California I was, as Mark Twain said, "surprised at how much Dad had learned."

Dad had good common sense, personal integrity and a calm disposition. But he never put in words that he loved me until he was in his later years. Men didn't do that then. He wasn't sentimental about things. He wasn't tight with his money, but he was conservative and was a good investor.

He certainly didn't agree with my wishes sometimes, but he knew I was strong-willed and eventually he became proud of me. We spent endless hours talking about fishing, spiritual things, the stock market, politics and Sweden. Of course, he made some mistakes with me, as dads are prone to do, but I overlook these, for he was a great role model, given his upbringing. I loved him very much and miss him a great deal.

G.A.

SIGNIFICANT PORTRAITS

MOTHER—EBBA O. E. ANDERSON

42) My mother, Ebba
70 Yrs old

My mom, Ebba Anderson[42], was a stay-at-home mom all her life with the exception of a very short stint at Crescent Tool. She would walk with me from our Newland Avenue home (near the present Hillcrest Baptist Church) down to Baker Street, where we would catch a street car, transfer to the Willard Street line, and go to see my grandma Brostrom on Swan Street on Swede Hill.

My mom loved ice-skating when she was young. There was a skating rink on the lake, maintained by the Lakewood firemen[43]. Sometimes Mom would skate there with other guys even though my dad was skating there, too. I couldn't figure that out.

My mom was a people person and loved parties and visiting others. Indeed, her whole Brostrom family would celebrate every birthday for the entire family. Later, during the summer months, the parties took place at the cottage. The men would play horseshoes and the women would talk about the next engagement or wedding, or just "big lady" talk.

Mom tended to be a perfectionist, which created a certain amount of misery and anxiety. She loved order and tradition. Invariably, Monday was washday, Tuesday was ironing day, Wednesday and Thursday were meeting "the girls" for lunch days, or having her hair done and going shopping. Friday was cleaning day.

She saw beauty in almost everything. She was an excellent cook. Geri told me more than once she felt closer to my mom than she did to her own. Mom was always riddled with worry and anxiety and yet she was a devoted Christian. She, like many, found it difficult to make the leap from anxiety to faith. She was my most avid supporter. She would secretly get me invited to play the violin or speak at various groups. She tried to manipulate my dad at times and many thought she was the boss of our household. This wasn't true. Dad would let her ramble and rave, then he would finally say, "That's enough. The answer is no." There was no moving him.

Mom and Dad were deeply in love and great companions. Their marriage lasted for 53 years before my dad passed away. On my mom's 80th birthday we had a party for her at our house, and more than 100 friends and relatives came! Some were former Sunday School students[44]. She was very well liked by many people.

Her love for my brother and me was well expressed and her love for her grandsons and her one great-grandchild, Nicholas, was also great. Her next great-grandchild, Nicolette, was one year old when my mom passed away, so she never got to know her. Had Mom's mind been alert, she would have been extremely happy because there had not been a girl in the Ludwig Anderson family for 116 years. Then, five years after Mom's death came a second great-granddaughter, Grace Elizabeth Anderson, bearing my initials. I can just see my mom doting on her precious great-grandchildren. A fourth great-grandchild, Harmony Joy Anderson, came into our hearts and home on March 26, 2004.

G.A.

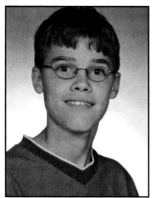

Nicholas 14 yrs

Nicolette - 10 years

Grace - 4 years

Harmony - 1 year

SIGNIFICANT PORTRAITS

GRANDPA AND GRANDMA

JOHN AND AUGUSTA BROSTROM

G randpa[52] and Grandma Brostrom[53] didn't play a big part in my life except through my mother. As adults they found Christ and were devoted Christians. They joined the Swedish Zion Mission Church (now Zion Covenant Church) in 1904 when the church was 10 years old.

52,53) John and Augusta Brostrom

Grandpa Brostrom was a stonemason; he built foundations all over town. The old Levant Wesleyan Church[54] is one example of his workmanship. He died in 1928 so neither my dad nor I knew him.

Grandma Brostrom always seemed tired and sick. She had had nine children, but one died in infancy. Several of the children, including my mom, were born on Swan Street. My grandpa, John Brostrom, I was told, built a house for them on Harris Avenue for when they retired, but Grandma wanted to stay where she was. With eight children to care for and a cow down on Harris Avenue, which she had to milk twice a day, she told my mom that she was worn out. She lived with us on Cole Avenue for a short time after both of my grandfathers died. She died of cancer when I was eight years old.

G.A.

54) Grandpa built the foundation for the old Levant Weslyan Church

SIGNIFICANT PORTRAITS

BROTHER—DANIEL N. ANDERSON

I had begged my parents for a baby brother or sister. I didn't want to be an only child. With World War II going on, my dad, who had a lot of energy, was working long hours at Crescent Tool, sometimes from 7:00 a.m. to 9:00 p.m. and Saturdays as well. He had saved a modest amount of money and, I guess, he felt he could afford another child to add to the one who had been his "depression baby."

56) Dan Anderson

So when I was 12 years old, my brother[56] was born on September 29, 1944. I was thrilled. I named him and helped feed him. When he was five years old, I left for North Park College. Therefore, I really didn't know my brother in my adulthood until I returned from California in 1963.

My brother and I were quite different. He was interested in biology—the woods, animals, fishing and hunting, sports, and unusual weather. He won a scholarship to the State University College at Fredonia, after having gone to Jamestown Community College for two years. He majored in biology and got his M.A. in that discipline. He taught at Dunkirk High School for a short time and then went to Westfield Academy. He now teaches at JCC.

It so happened that I had at least two of Dan's former students at JCC. They said something like this: "We had a teacher at Westfield Academy whose name was Anderson. He has a teaching style very much like yours. He tells stories to make learning practical and to make it stick in your mind." I asked what their teacher's first name was and they said "Daniel." I said, "That's my brother!"

So even though we have different interests, we teach about the same way. Dan has had numerous awards for his teaching and has done scholarly research on Chautauqua Lake, which has been published. We get along very well and enjoy each other's company.

He got married at age 48, for the first time. I had the privilege of doing the vows with him and his bride, Shauna. Her father was president of the State University College at Brockport for many years. He is Dr. Albert Brown and his wife is Marjorie. They live close to Dan and Shauna on Lake Chautauqua. Dan is as hooked on the lake as I am.

G.A

FISH TALES

(Gordon Anderson speaking)

n the story of my life, many things are important—my work, especially my teaching; my two very fine sons; my political career; my ministry; my success as a businessman— and yet, perhaps, nothing tops my long love affair with Chautauqua Lake.

There have already been accounts of my relationship to fishing on Lake Chautauqua—in my portrait of my dad and in Fred Falldine's memoir. But these accounts haven't yet said it all, and I want my chance to chime in.

One of the most important things about my childhood at Connelly Park was that I loved to fish and I was either swimming in the lake with the other kids or with my cousin Carolyn, or if I wasn't swimming, I was taking my grandpa's old flat-bottom boat out (by this time he had died), and we would fish. We would go for bass and I remember one time fishing for bass in the rain with my cousin Howard Larson, and I got a three-pounder and Howard didn't get anything and I felt very bad about that. But he and I caught beautiful sunfish up in Hadley's Bay, big and colorful, which we would eat for dinner. During the depression, that was the thing—to eat fish. I got tired of some of them, but we had fish often.

As I got older, my attention turned to my dad's way of fishing. He would do a lot of casting, in weeds. And then I became interested in muskellunge and trolling. Muskies were pretty numerous in 1948. (See chart below.) That year I had 18 muskies in the boat! Most of them were too small to keep. But I did catch a large muskie when I was about 40 years old. My largest fish[62] was 22 pounds and 44 inches long. When I got into the county legislature, I gave up fishing. Now that I'm retired, I've gone back to it a little bit. And I take my grandchildren fishing, too.

62) 22 lb. Muskie

Of course my best fish story is when I caught the 22-pound muskie. I caught it on a bass plug and my dad said, "You're taking it in too fast. Get the muskie tired before you try to get it in the boat." Just when I got it up to the boat, my dad had the landing net under him, but the fish shook himself loose. Fortunately the net was there. And my dad said, "See, I told you so. You're too anxious." But I said, "Yeah, but I got him." (But I wouldn't have had him if my dad hadn't been there.) One of our neighbors got one that was 42 pounds, and it was great sport. You'd come in in the evening and all the neighbors would come over to see what you got.

One time Freddy Falldine (or was it Dick Hunt?) and I fished in the Watson Canal. The fish were trapped in there because of the low water in the lake—but we got our boat in there and were catching fish right and left. Then a fish was hooked on my line and I pulled hard, but no fish. That rascal had pulled my hook off and escaped. I had to quit. But in a few minutes my partner caught a sunfish and, lo and behold, my hook was in his mouth! He took the hook off and gave it to me. I tied it back on my line and kept on fishing.

We were trolling near Whitney's Crib and I caught a monster! It went one way and then another. When I finally reeled it in it was a fossil rock with what looked like a wormhole in it. My hook went in the tiny hole! Oh well, you can't win them all; sometimes you can't win anything.

Now Chautauqua Lake, as I view it, is no longer a fisherman's paradise. Until the summer people are gone it's too hard to fish, by trolling, because there are so many powerboats and water skiers and those little jet skis, which make it very difficult. When September comes and the visitors go home and the kids go back to school—then you can have the lake pretty much to yourself again. And that's a good time to fish muskellunge or bass.

Fish Stocked in Chautauqua Lake, New York 1944-1953

Type of Fish	1944	1945	1946	1947	1948**	1949	1950	1951	1952	1953
Muskellunge Fry	4,120,000	2,000,000	2,185,000	5,017,150	5,277,000	2,559,000	3,809,000	—	4,055,000	2,143,000
Muskellunge Fingerlings*	—	4,305 (8.0)	5,317 (8.0)	9,258 (7.5) 3,833 (7.0)	220 (12.0)	3,989 (9.5)	2,372 (7.0) 8,349 (8.5)	4,686 (10.5) 350 (11.0) 6,247 (5.0) 4,117 (5.5)	7,285 (1.5) 43,297 (1.0) 2,654 (8.5)	16,000 (1.0) 4,336 (8.0)
Small Mouth Bass Fry	—	—	—	—	—	—	—	—	—	—
Small Mouth Bass Fingerlings*	24,577	7,549	11,300	1,800	16,966	1,818	40,027	28,080	555	44,371 36 (11.5)

* average length, in inches, is given in parenthesis   **Banner year for Muskellunge

23

PHOTO GALLERY-1

3) P.P. Wallenström 1838-1917

4) Grandfather John Brostrom - on right with shovel, John's brother, C. Oscar Brostrom kneeling, left front by wheelbarrow, Great Grandfather Gustaf Brostrom, behind wheel barrow

5) Gordon and his father, Edwin

7) Jamestown City Market

8) "Sweetie Pie"

9) Gordon with Patty and Dick Hunt

10) Gordon and Carolyn with dog Pepper

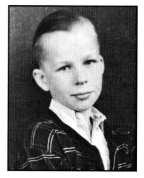

11) Howard Larson

PHOTO GALLERY-1

12) Miss Gretzler's First Grade

13A) Gordon going to school

14) Gordon as concert master
and Paul Sparrman, a lifelong
friend

14a) JHS Orchestra

15) Ebba Goranson

17) John Anderson

20) Janet, Gordon,
Freddie Falldine

PHOTO GALLERY-1

22) Andersson Farm, Ryggåsen, near Vimmerby, Sweden

23) Great grandparents Mr. and Mrs. Peter Andersson

24) Houseboat shed similar to Grandpa Anderson's

25) Rolling the shanty to Connelly Park

26) Grandpa Louie and Vic Olson leveling the lot at Connelly Park

27) Cow Fence to lake

28) Trolly that ran past Connelly Park

28A) Cottage Receipt

29) Ice storage House in Stow

PHOTO GALLERY-1

30a) Ludwig and a Catch

30b) Ludwig seining for Blue Nose Chubs (now extinct) for bass bait

32) Grandma Hilfred working for rich people in Sweden before she emigrated

33) Grandparents, Ludwig and Hilfred Anderson at Connelly Park

34) Edwin, age two in Sweden

35) A sample of Grandma's handiwork

37) Dad's first motor boat

37a) Dad and 32 lb muskie

38) 1939 World's Fair New York City

39) Crescent Tool Workers 1922. My Dad was 16 years old

40) Dad, as foreman of Die Dept.

43) Skating on Lake in Lakewood

44) One of Ebba's Sunday School classes

49) Ice skating on "Sumpin" Pond Willard St. Ext (1920s) Near Ebba's girlhood home

50) Mom on Mother's Day 1953

51) One of last pictures of Ebba at the Gerry Rodeo as if she was saying "Goodbye"

57) Gordon and little brother, Danny

57A) Gordon and brother Dan work on a carpentry project

58) Dan learning to fish

59) Brother Dan driving "Sweetie Pie"

60) Dan always liked hiking

61) Dan with his muskie

CHAPTER TWO

A POX ON CHICKEN POX

I n 1950, 18-year-old Gordon Anderson left his home base in Jamestown, left his prized boat, Sweetie Pie, left his beloved brother, only age five, his beloved parents and grandmother, his friends, his security, and his adored Chautauqua Lake, and went away to college.

2) Family business on Third Street where I worked summers

Millions of young people have done a similar thing year after year after year. It is always traumatic, often very difficult, sometimes unfortunate, but usually eventually for the best. For Gordon, it was "the beginning of the rest of his life," which, as a result, has turned out pretty well.

He was the first of his family to go to college—a not unusual situation for Americans of his generation, especially when their parents had been first-generation offspring of immigrants. All the way through his elementary school and high school years he had done well academically; he was widely active in extracurricular activities, even winning awards[1], especially for his music. He didn't want, nor did his father want for him, to continue a tradition of working as a factory-worker; nor did he want, as his father wanted for him, to buy, on installment, a partnership in Brostrom-Conner Shoes[2], a shoe store his uncles owned. He had what are usually described as "higher ambitions." He wanted to go to college. But that took money, and where would the money come from?

Though his parents were, by his own description, devoted and loving, neither of them, he felt, valued higher education very much. His father had dropped out of school at 16 to earn a living; his mother graduated from high school. Following the model of most wives and mothers in the first half of the

20th century, she concentrated on home and family and was not overly in favor of higher education.

Gordon, therefore, faced a dilemma. Through his high school activities as a musical performer, member of the J.H.S. debate team, starting a J.I.M. club in 1947 which met weekly at a neighborhood church, and other things, he was well-known in Jamestown. Algot J. E. Larson, President of Art Metal, Jamestown's largest manufacturing plant, and a member of Gordon's church, at one point asked him if he planned to go to North Park College. Gordon said yes, but he had no money. Larson told him: "You go. And if you ever need money, let me know."

When Edwin Anderson heard of this, it embarrassed him, and he acknowledged that Gordon should go on to more schooling, but he'd have to earn his way at least by half and he, his father, would provide the other half. He said, "You'll be lucky if you get through North Park."

Thus Gordon went off—to North Park College in Chicago[3] "because it was the denominational school of the Evangelical Covenant Church, and that's how I happened to go there."

At the end of two years, he earned an Associate Degree, but with great difficulty. Money was a constant problem. He was forced to work at a variety of jobs for as much time as he could manage in order to keep himself afloat. During the two years, he worked at an electric blanket company; a map company; at Dutch Boy Paints printing labels; at the Swedish Covenant Hospital scrubbing the stairs, and sometimes in x-ray, putting x-rays on microfilm; and he also sold shoes to immigrant and Jewish people "down on Lawrence Avenue."

In his second year at North Park, his "sister" Carolyn came there as a freshman, as did his friend Paul Sparrman. During the summers he worked at Crescent Tool, Art Metal, and then, later, at his uncles' shoe store.

"Life was hard for me," he said. "It did not come easy. But I had some things going for me. I did have a father and mother who loved me very much. And I had a grandmother who loved me very much. And I also had the Lord in my heart, who was looking out for me, and I claimed His promise that He would never leave me nor forsake me."

The pressure of constantly needing money and of using much of his out-of-class time for work made it difficult to keep up his grades. He was housed in an apartment with six other young men, "but," he said, "there was always someone who wasn't interested in studying and who always wanted to goof off," and that made studying difficult in the small time he had for it; and, he said, "Sometimes it was me!"

He was majoring in a pre-theology program, and took a lot of liberal arts courses, including psychology. Still, he did get through and got the degree, although a bad case of chicken pox prevented him from attending the graduation ceremony. His parents had come to attend and took a picture

4) North Park Seminary

of where he should have been in the ceremonial line.

"I do think I got a good education at North Park," Gordon says.

The next step was either to go on to another college for further study, or to go to North Park's Seminary[4]. Acting on his considerable interest in serving Christ, and on what he felt was a call towards the ministry, Gordon interviewed for a spot in the seminary and was accepted.

At the end of that third year[5], his father finally told him he would completely fund two more years of college if he would go to Houghton College, back in New York State. What a change! But Gordon's ambition prevailed: he wanted to see the world, or at least more of it, and he accepted, instead, a year of ministerial internship at the First Covenant Church in San Francisco, California.

For his service as youth pastor at the church, he was to receive $100 a month, which had to cover rent, food, and visiting the sick. Very quickly he found, even in 1953, $100 wasn't enough. So when his internship was over, he found himself once again selling shoes, in a Chandler shoe store in a shopping mall—a high-volume operation where Gordon, who by now was pretty good at moving shoes, soon proved his mettle.

The ministerial work was hard, since he was the first intern/assistant they had ever had, and the person under whom he worked was not particularly helpful. And the parishioners, though good people, were not aware of the needs of a young, single youth director for companionship and hospitality. He spent the first Thanksgiving alone with Ingrid—a cat he got from the SPCA—and the first Christmas almost alone, except that he was invited to the home of one family where he watched them opening their presents and felt even more lonely.

At the end of the internship year, he left the church, though he remained in San Francisco, where he enrolled in San Francisco City College, intent on finishing his next college degree. By then, too, his skill as a shoe salesman had caught the attention of Harry Parlow, who operated the Joseph Magnin shoe concession, which was a high-market operation patronized by women looking for glamorous, expensive shoes. Customers were movie stars, show girls, society women, ladies of the night—many for whom quality and glamour were important. Among Gordon's customers at the Magnin store were Willie May's wife, the governor's wife, and Eva Gabor. He also dated a couple of the models employed by the store.

It happened that Parlow's wife had come to Chandler's to buy slippers, which the Magnin store did not carry, and had been so impressed with Gordon's salesmanship that she told her husband about it.

Parlow offered Gordon a part-time job at full-time salary if he would promise to work for him for three years after receiving his college degree. Gordon took the offer and, for the first time in his fledgling "on-his-own" career, money ceased to be a problem.

At that time you could go to school free in California if you had a driver's license. All you had to pay was $28 plus books. On the advice of a young woman he knew, he switched to San Francisco State College, where he blossomed as a student, earning his Bachelor of Arts degree in

6) A more reliable car

1956. He completed his master's degree there as well. He did student teaching and then began to look for a permanent teaching job.

In the meantime, every summer but one, he drove home to New York State to be with his family and enjoy the pleasures of "Sweetie Pie," the lake and the home turf he loved. However, he always also got a summer job, either at Crescent Tool, Art Metal, or selling shoes, to make sure the trips back and forth could be managed. He had by this time traded the 1948 car his father had sold him for $800 for a newer Buick[6] that could be relied on for the rugged trips across the continent. Cars had no air conditioning as yet and the desert crossings were brutal. There was no interstate highway system across the entire country as there is today. To help finance the trips, he always advertised for riders to accompany him and share expenses.

By the time he was 25, his mother, concerned about what she regarded as his too-carefree, slightly irresponsible life, was urging him to settle down. "When are you going to find a wife?" she asked.

Months later, he entered into an unofficial engagement with Donna Anderson, a woman he'd met in California, but then, in the summer of 1957, his cousin Lucille Johnson introduced him to Geraldine Brown. He wasn't sure at first that Geri was for him, but he knew the other woman wasn't the one. He eventually realized Geraldine, as he put it, "was made for me[7] and I was made for her." They were married on July 26, 1958 [8], and then returned to California.

Shortly thereafter Gordon was offered a job teaching in Arcata, California[9], 300 miles north of San Francisco. The position was to teach History[10] and Psychology in the high school. He accepted. By the time they moved, in a U-Haul truck, Geri was expecting their first child, Daniel, who was born in Arcata. Gordon taught there for four years, the first of which they spent in a rented house, and then they bought a similar place[11] expecting, perhaps, that they would be staying permanently.

The Arcata School[12] was on double sessions because half the school had been condemned. Gordon started teaching at 6:50 A.M. every weekday. Some of the students had come 40 miles to school on a bus.

"One day," Gordon relates, "a kid fell asleep—he just laid his head down on the desk. I decided to let him sleep just for the fun of it. We didn't have our own classrooms. We had to keep changing. So I just told the class 'be quiet when you go out.' When the next class came in, I said, 'Be quiet, there's someone sleeping.' And I told the next teacher who was going to have that room that there was someone sleeping. The boy woke up in the middle of the next class and he couldn't figure out where he was and who the teacher was and what had happened to him. I have to say, he never fell asleep again. But I just sort of felt sorry for him and others who came 40 miles by bus."

While still living in San Francisco, Gordon and Geri had participated in "planting" a new church, later to become Grace Covenant, with Gordon as a willing, unpaid, interim pastor. Through the process of becoming an intern at First Covenant Church, Gordon was licensed to perform ministerial duties, though he wasn't yet ordained. Thus, by renewing his license, he was able to lead putting the new congregation on its feet. When they left for Arcata, the church was stable enough that its new building was being realized, it had a permanent membership, and it could hire a permanent pastor. "I felt a little like Moses, never to see the Promised Land," said Gordon.

In Arcata the Andersons once again set out to start a new church[14]. A small group of people rented the Seventh Day Adventist church, and attracted 40 people or so. The effort never achieved the stability and permanence they hoped for, and in the end the people voted to give it up.

By this time (1962), they were both feeling pulls back to Chautauqua County: they were tired of the annual summer "commute" back and forth, though coming home in the summer was expected, partly because the four grandparents[15,16] wanted to see their grandchild. Yet, it was becoming increasingly difficult to finance these annual trips on a teacher's salary, which was low at that time ($5200 with an M.A., paid over nine months, one check a month!). Moreover, Gordon had proved to be very allergic to the molds in Northern California, and moving seemed a good idea. Finally, they were homesick, and with one child already and another on the way, they felt they should return to their roots. So they put their house up for sale.

Through all of this, the move felt right, because both Gordon and Geri sustained a never-ending faith that Gordon's was a life devoted to and watched over by their God. Just as they were scheduled to leave Arcata, a Christian couple who seemed to be the perfect buyers for their Arcata house came along and made just the right offer, in just the right way. Again, Gordon and Geri felt God was indeed pointing them in the right direction.

Gordon says, "We had loved the drives between Jamestown and Arcata including across Canada, even though they had become burdensome. We crossed 24 times (12 round trips). We traveled the southern route, the central routes over the mountains, and the northern route over the years. Our country is so beautiful. If we could write a travel log, it would make its own book. But this time we took the most central and shortest route. In those days we didn't hit an expressway until Elkhart, Indiana, so it was all on two-lane roads."

Though Geri's doctor was seriously against a car trip across the country in her state of pregnancy—seven months along by now—they settled on a system of stopping every hour so she could walk and prevent troubles. It was a very long trip home from Arcata to Driftwood, but it was done.

Once back at Driftwood, they settled into the next phase of their lives, which included the birth of their second son, David[17]. Gordon began teaching at Jamestown High School and later at Jamestown Community College[18]. Almost immediately the "Driftwood Campaign" began; and down the road were the years as a politician, which made him a force to be reckoned with in Chautauqua County.

SIGNIFICANT PORTRAITS

MY WIFE—GERALDINE BROWN ANDERSON

I n the summer of 1957, my cousin, Lucille Johnson, arranged for me to meet Geri in the Brostrom-Conner shoe store on East Third Street in Jamestown. Geri[19] and I went to lunch the next day and dated each day after that until I had to return to California.

19) Geri Anderson

Geraldine Brown was from Sugar Grove, PA[20], the daughter of Lloyd and Florence Brown, now both deceased. She is the middle child in a family of five siblings. She had moved to Jamestown, where she worked for Universal CIT Corporation, a subsidiary of the parent company CIT Corp. She quickly picked up my love for the lake. We went canoeing, and rode in my boat "Sweetie Pie." Our love was growing.

I returned to California, work and school. After a few months I invited her to come out to California to see if she liked the west. In December of 1957, CIT Corp. transferred her to the San Francisco office in the financial district and she rented an apartment from Bob and Mary Ann Peterson, who were close friends of mine from my First Covenant internship days. The problem was that the distance from where I lived and worked was a very long drive away from where she worked and lived. We did manage to see each other at least once a week.On a windy, cold night early in 1958, high on a hill in San Francisco overlooking the ocean, I asked her to marry me and she said, "yes," and I gave her a diamond. I was shaking, partly because I was nervous, partly because it was cold, and partly because I was afraid I would drop the ring! We were married on July 26, 1958, in Zion Covenant Church in Jamestown.

As time went on, Geri was anxious to do what I liked to do, such as the lake, later taking trips to Sweden, learning the Swedish language (she speaks it better than I do). She has been a wonderful caring wife, kind and gentle. We've never cheated on each other. We like the same things—music, our beliefs about God and other activities. She was also a stay-at-home mother for Dan and Dave and is a loving grandmother to Nicholas, Nicolette, Grace and Harmony. She is also a superb cook.

I could not have found a better wife, even if I had drawn up specifications. My "old girlfriend" in California now says, "you are very fortunate to have her—to put up with you!" Geri keeps me in line by saying, "You are educated beyond your intelligence," or"You may be chairman of this or president of that, but you are just plain ole' Gord to me." (I hope she is just kidding about my intelligence!)

Geri loves needlework, acrylic painting, and her flower gardens. She stitched the hardest counted cross-stitch piece I could find in Denmark's Eva Rosenstand needlework shop. It is a harbor scene of Old Stockholm in 1693[21], measuring 43 inches by 15 inches, worked on 30-count linen. It took over 1500 hours to complete. It is beautiful.

G.A.

SIGNIFICANT PORTRAITS

EVANGELIST JIMMIE DAVIS

immie Davis[22] was a very talented man: He sang with the Long Beach Symphony Orchestra, was a trumpeter, and was chosen many times as a song leader by major evangelists traveling the country in those days. He also liked kids.

22) Jimmie Davis

I met him in 1946, shortly after the Wyrtsen campaign at Jamestown High School. Davis was having meetings as an evangelist at Kidder Church, one block from where I lived on Cole Avenue in Jamestown. He used magic object lessons to convey Bible stories, sang, and encouraged the audience to sing too. He was a very generous man who gave me many magic tricks, most of which I still have. He taught me how to use them.

I went to schools, lodges, and various other groups and did magic with Bible stories, together with playing my violin. I could have been out many nights in the week, but, since I was only 15 or 16, I had to limit myself because of homework. I also had two close friends, Paul Sparrman[23], who also played the violin, and Wesley Chall[24], who played the piano. The three of us were asked out continually[25], playing classical music and light music for dinners and church functions.

But then I got an idea: Why not start a J.I.M. (Jesus is Mine) Club[26]? Paul Sparrman and I asked the pastor of Kidder Church if we could use the church once a week on Fridays to sing, play our violins and present gospel magic[27]. The church board ruled "Yes."

We made a sign, which I hung outside the church before school every Friday. A lot of kids came. The impetus and ideas Davis gave me helped me to become more self-assured and known in the Jamestown area.

Davis and I took several rides in "Sweetie Pie" to discuss his dream of a summer camp on Lake Chautauqua. His dream came true in 1954 and he purchased a tract of land about one mile west of Midway Park to develop what is now J.I.M. Club of America. A former J.I.M. Club boy, Brian Stapley, is the Director of the camp.

Jimmie Davis died in 1981.

P.S. As boyhood pals, Wes, Paul and I had nicknames for each other. We called Wes "Doctor", (he became a dentist); we referred to Paul as "Rev.", (he became a pastor); and they called me "Professor", which I ultimately became.

G.A.

PHOTO GALLERY-2

1) Arion Foundation Award
for Music

3) Old Main at North Park College, Chicago

5)First Covenant Church on
Delores St. in Francisco

7) Years before we knew each other. Ironically these were taken at
Murphys 5 & 10 Cent Store and we're about the same age

8) The start of our life
together

9) Downtown Arcata, CA

10) A tattered flag from the
War for Independence

11) Our newly purchased home, Arcata. Same design as our rented house

12) Arcata High School

13) Artist's drawing of Grace Covenant Church, So. San Francisco

14) Arcata congregation on the steps of our rented church

15) Grandma Anderson says a tearful "Goodbye" to her first grandchild before he returns to California

16) Danny gets a 4"Crescent wrench just like Grandpa's big wrench

17) Our second son David, 9 mo. old

PHOTO GALLERY-2

18) Gordon outside the L.I.S.S. building at JCC

20) Picnic at Alleghany State Park to meet her family

21) Geri's counted cross stitch masterpiece. Old Stockholm, 1693

23) Gordon and Paul Sparrman conducting the first JIM Club

24) My lifelong friend, Wes Chall

26) The Jim club boys

25) Our instrumental trio featured in an ad

27) The young Magician at work

40

CHAPTER THREE

TO KNOW IS NOTHING AT ALL;
TO IMAGINE IS EVERYTHING

fter three years of teaching in Arcata, Gordon felt the rather normal career wanderlust that affects many. He had already achieved tenure and, though he was happy in teaching, he wanted to experience it in other environments. And, as has been discussed previously, he and Geri were beginning to succumb to homesickness and a desire to return to their home territory, which for them was the Jamestown, New York area and Chautauqua Lake.

Still, to hedge his bets, he applied for teaching jobs in high schools in three places: Mill Valley in Marin County, California; San Raphael, California; and Jamestown, New York. As he was considering the job offered in Mill Valley, a teacher friend advised him that, as a parent of a young child, he should not move there because, in addition to housing being so expensive in the area, there was also a prevalence of drug trade and it would not be a good place to raise a child. The same was true for San Raphael. Such advice, in the early 1960s already, was frightening for a parent. Moreover, as for church work, the superintendent of the California Covenant Church Conference, Gordon Nelson, advised Gordon that there was no opportunity to start a church in San Raphael.

But the application to Jamestown proved successful and Gordon and Geri set about finding a house in the Chautauqua Lake area. A couple of years earlier, on the 4th of July, they had been invited to go through the new home of Judith Peterson, a neighbor to Gordon's parents. They very much admired the location higher up on Driftwood Road, and the panoramic view of Chautauqua Lake. It was not Connelly Park, but it was beautiful. However, the house was not for sale at that time. When they finally decided it was time to move back, the house on Driftwood[1,2] came up for sale. Once again, it seemed that God was making the decision easier and the direction crystal clear.

So, in 1963, the Andersons made the final drive, using the biggest U-Haul trailer available to cross the country back to their home area. Gordon was taking a cut in salary in the new job, but they knew living costs would be less and it would eventually even out.

In Jamestown, Gordon had contracted to teach social studies. Over the next four years he taught American History, Sociology, Economics, Ancient History, and Political Science, and he started a Psychology program, adding it to the Jamestown High School curriculum. It was approved by the school board and became a very popular course. He also once again achieved tenure and was not afraid for the future.

However, in 1967 he got a call from Professor Harry Bridges, chairman of the Social Sciences Division at Jamestown Community College. Bridges had taken note, through students, of the fact that Gordon was teaching psychology at the high school at the level of what was being taught at JCC, and he invited Gordon to apply to teach at the college.

Then, according to Gordon, began one of those dances not unfamiliar to people applying for employment: the JCC administration was not forthcoming with an offer of the job. As it happened, though, Gordon at the same time had been invited to come back to California to help form a social sciences division at a new school, the College of the Redwoods near Eureka, California.

"It was a great opportunity," Gordon said. "But our house on Driftwood Road was still tied up in the highway business [the rerouting of the expressway] and I felt we had moved from California once to come home, and so . . .I pulled the letter [from Eureka] out of my pocket and showed it to the JCC administrators and I was hired immediately as an assistant professor. When I left I was so flustered I forgot which door I had come in and I walked into the President's washroom!

"Another gaffe I made occurred when I was invited by the trustees, along with other new teachers, to a dinner at Moonbrook Country Club. I was milling around talking and someone bumped my arm and the punch in my hand went down Mrs. Clyde Carnahan's back. I was so embarrassed! But Katherine Carnahan was so gracious. Someone told me I couldn't have picked anyone more forgiving. I noticed, however, she stayed away from me for the rest of the evening. "And I loved JCC. I had great experiences there and I loved the students."[3] In fact, he adds, "teaching was the love of my life."[4]

Over a career of 35 or so years, including public school teaching, Gordon figures he has taught probably 14,000 students, and he still runs into some every now and then who tell him how much his classes meant to them—that he "taught them how to think," he always kept things interesting, and that various courses like his Stress and Coping helped them to mature and handle their personal lives.

He also loved to tease his students and in turn he got it back. One day, a female student came to class with a cup of coffee. She spilled it and Gordon said, "How does it feel to be so uncoordinated? You'd better go get some paper towels." At that moment he knocked his own coffee over, and the students cheered. "It served me right," he said.

There are many more stories he recalls. One day he walked by a class-room where John Collins taught. Seeing that John was out of the room, he dropped a piece of chalk in the coffee cup on the desk. It turned out that John Hearn was using the room that day and John Collins was in another room. When Gordon asked Collins how his coffee tasted he said, "Fine." Then Gordon learned he had put chalk in Hearn's cup. Embarrassed, he went to apologize to Hearn, who said the students kept asking how his coffee tasted. But John Collins, the intended victim, got even with Gordon. He would tease Gordon, complimenting him on a suit and then say, "They're coming back in style again." One suit, which Gordon often wore to the County Legislature, Collins dubbed a "swindlesuit." Collins would also put his junk mail in Gordon's mailbox.

Among the courses and programs Gordon developed at JCC were Abnormal Psychology, Community Service in the Social Sciences (which led directly to the Human Services program at JCC), the innovative Stress and Coping (which became a very popular course), The Psychology of Human Behavior, and Profiles and Ideas of Prominent Psychologists since 1879.

In addition, he started the Swedish Exchange Program, which was sup-ported by local residents and organizations of Swedish descent, and which thrived from 1983 to 1994. About 85 students were involved during this period and every one of them said in a questionnaire that it changed their lives and broadened their worldview.

Gordon also broke out of the usual mold for community college teach-ing, which did not emphasize research to a great extent, by getting National Science Foundation grants. The first was for study at Claremont Graduate School in California[5] in 1966, which he described as "the best learning experi-ence I had ever had." In 1968 he went to Florida State University, where he conceived a research project, which led to further NSF grants for JCC to sup-port establishment of a psychology lab through which students engaged in significant research. In this regard, he invented a modified "skinner" box by which a rat from his rat colony could distinguish warm and cool by touching its nose to a series of warm or cool moving containers on the wall of the box.

The rat would go to a "warm" feeder or a "cool" feeder for reinforce-ment. Gradually, the variation of the "warm" and "cool" temperatures was reduced, bringing the temperatures closer together until the rat was able to distinguish a mere 2 degree threshold. Previous studies elsewhere had shown the rats could distinguish as low as an 11 degree threshold. The out-come of this study was very significant as far as pure science is concerned.

Debra Lawson[6], a freshman student, had trained the rat and Gordon, her mentor, urged her to present a paper of the findings at the Fifth Intercampus Psychology Conference held at Oswego State College. She demonstrated her work in several classes at JCC. She won statewide recogni-tion and has since become a Psychologist for the Army.

Eventually, Gordon was granted a second sabbatical leave to pursue graduate study and he earned his Ph.D. in Higher Education and Psychology from the University of Buffalo in 1988.

Throughout his teaching career Gordon had consistent high evaluations from his students and recommendations from his peers for promotions and merit raises. He went from assistant professor to full professor faster than anyone else, with the exception of one other person.

7) Main Building at SVF

One honor eluded him—the State University of New York award for Excellence in Teaching. This was not because he wasn't nominated or deserving, for supporters testified to both; but rather, because of a technicality, since he was serving as a division chairman at the time of the nomination and was ruled out on the ground that department chairs were not eligible for the teaching award. "The Dean," Gordon recalled, "threw the petition, which had been presented to him, initiated by the students, and containing many, many signatures, into the wastebasket in my presence. That hurt!"

As facilitator of the Swedish exchange program, with Södra Vatterbygdens Folkhögskola (SVF)[7] in Jönköping, he set up the program in Sweden, and also took on the responsibility of finding host homes for the Swedish students when they came to Jamestown. He hosted students each year in his own home as well. He also studied in Sweden at Uppsala University and taught at the University of Stockholm (see his commentaries below). The involvement with Sweden added an additional richness to his teaching, since it reinforced the value of international study and of connection between immigrant communities, such as Jamestown, and their home countries. He also tried three times to establish a Sister City relationship between Jamestown and Jönköping-Huskvarna, but the Swedish city was not interested. Gordon did, however, become Lidköping's[8] ambassador to Jamestown.

Part of the satisfaction Gordon felt in his teaching career had to do with colleagues. Professor Harry Bridges, who brought him to teach at JCC in the first place, became a good friend and serious mentor. The late John Collins, professor of anthropology, who came to JCC in the same "class" as Gordon, became his closest colleague.

In a letter of support for Gordon in 1984, Collins wrote: "I have observed his teaching on many occasions and I am fully aware of his many long-term contributions to this institution . . . .Gordon is an excellent teacher, combining lecture and discussion, and always draws full classes of interested students. He endeavors to make his material relevant to their interests and lives and personalizes the data with his own varied experiences. . . .Above all, to my mind, are his contributions to our Swedish Exchange Program. This highly successful project is solely the result of his efforts—in fundraising, recruiting, organizing, and administering . . . ."

Also, relevant to the exchange program, JCC President Paul Benke wrote a letter to Jennie Vimmerstedt[9], who had sent a contribution from the Norden Women's Club for the Swedish program, saying: "Gordon Anderson has done a magnificent job in getting our Swedish Exchange Program under-way. He has singlehandedly made a reality of a personal dream."

Others praised the program as well, including many of the students who participated in it. One wrote: "The time I spent at SVF and on the differ-ent travels with the school were wonderful learning experiences as well as some of the most special times in my life." From another: "This pro-gram is excellent. I think that the experiences I'm having now will affect the rest of my life." And still a third wrote: "It was hard to speak Swedish at first but now we have become braver and the Swedes are beginning to speak less English [in order to help us]. Our meals here at SVF[10] are great; it is as if it was Christmas dinner every day."

9) Paul Benke, Jennie Vimmerstedt, Gordon, Unkown, Ulf Beijbom from the Emigrant Museum, Vaxjö, Sweden

Gordon himself evaluated the exchange program in his doctoral disser-tation. Among his conclusions were his findings that Americans changed their attitudes greatly about their own country, the world, and the countries they visited, while the Swedes' attitudes did not shift so dramatically; and that the expectations of the students from both countries were met by the exchange program.

Gordon served Jamestown Community College in other ways during his tenure. For several years he was chairman of his division and was lauded by those who worked with him for his executive style and good time manage-ment, for listening and for being supportive, for initiating creative solutions, and for his ability to organize and get people to pull together—all qualities which he had already demonstrated in such efforts as the Driftwood cam-paign, and which would stand him in good stead in his other pursuits.

In many ways, Gordon's JCC career was special, and uniquely produc-tive. It was with great reluctance that he finally gave it up, after serious com-plications from elective surgery, in 1994, when he officially retired. At the time of his retirement, he was chairman of the planning committee for the remod-eling of the science building.

Then, again, he testified to his love for teaching, as he still does today, looking back at his many and varied endeavors.

UPPSALA UNIVERSITY

Summer 1992

T his was a program for which you had to apply. When I was accepted, Geri insisted on going with me because she didn't want any Swedish girls washing my underclothes. My courses included Swedish Language (ironically, the teacher was never able to learn English), Swedish Literature and Swedish History, both of which were taught in English along with some Swedish. It was hard for me; I think I was too old. My dad spoke beautiful Swedish; my mom spoke "swinglish," but most of what I knew was when they talked in Swedish when I was a boy so I wouldn't know what they were saying. I learned quickly that part of the language! My Grandma Anderson also taught me some phrases. Of course, Swedish is the official language of heaven.

UPPSALA UNIVERSITY
THE UNIVERSITY
BUILDING

11) Uppsala University

Uppsala is a beautiful university town and the university was the first or second one founded in Sweden. There is a running debate as to which one was first, Lund University or Uppsala.

Most people in Uppsala, whether 8 or 80 years old, ride bicycles or walk to town. The largest and most beautiful Cathedral[12] in all of Scandinavia is there.

Our class, of which I was the oldest, had wonderful field trips on Saturdays. We visited old Viking burial grounds[13] and runic stones; Rottneros Park, which is a display of magnificent outdoor sculptures; and Dalarna, which is considered to be the most beautiful part of Sweden. We also visited the home of Swedish novelist, Selma Lagerlöf, who was the first woman to receive a Nobel Prize; and Forsmark[14], a town near the site of a spent atomic fuel repository.

Forsmark grabbed my attention. It is like some of James Bond's 007 movies. You take a bus and go way underground until you are under the Baltic Sea! We have sailed over this place many times and never knew this huge cavern existed. Why was it made? Because Sweden has several atomic plants for electricity and the spent fuel is brought under the Baltic for storage. I got out of the bus and walked up some stairs and looked through some very thick glass and saw the spent rods.

Uppsala broadened my understanding of past Viking exploits as well as of modern-day Sweden. Geri and I had a wonderful time there, even though her participation in the program was somewhat limited because of University rules.

Uppsala University was founded in 1477 and is the oldest university in the Nordic countries. Versatile scientists like Olof Rudbeck, Anders Celsius and Carl von Linné laid the foundations for the research which has ever since attracted international attentions. With its faculties – Theology, Law, Medicine, Pharmacy, Arts Social Sciences and Mathmatics – Natural Sciences – Uppsala University offers many options within education and research.

-Courtesy Uppsala University Promotional Data

G.A.

STOCKHOLM'S UNIVERSITET

Winter Semester—1996

A wonderful opportunity was offered to me to be a visiting professor at the University of Stockholm in Sweden.[15] The offer was extended for the winter semester of 1995, which was to be my sabbatical leave from JCC; however, for reasons I will explain later, it was delayed until the winter semester of 1996.

15) Psychology Institute - the building where I taught

We, Geri and I, lived in university housing while we were there. It was very close to the bus line, which ultimately connected with the underground tunnel, or Tunnelbana. The underground system goes all over the city, north, south, east and west, so it is possible to go just about anyplace and then connect with a bus line, if necessary, to reach your destination. One day we decided to ride the entire route and get off at every stop, which you can do all for one fare by asking for a transfer. Our intent was to view what is known as the world's longest art exhibition.[16] Every station is decorated in a very different way, sometimes with inlaid colored tiles and sometimes painted. It is not graffiti or the work of kids with nothing to do but deface public property. It is intentionally done, making each stop a delight and I'm sure those who ride all the time can identify their stop by the artwork without even looking for a name. Even though the system is called the underground, it goes both above and below the ground, depending on the location. The largest part is, however, below ground level, running under churches and buildings and under the center of town, even under water in some places. On days when I wasn't too busy I went, via the underground tunnel, to the island of Lidingö where the Covenant Seminary is located and I read and studied in the library.

The Covenant Church in Stockholm[17] is, indeed, a unique structure. Seven Covenant churches merged to form the one church in the city. They were required to purchase an entire city block. It includes the church, with services in both Swedish and English languages, shops, a hotel and an underground sports complex. There is signage in the foyer pointing to all of these venues.

While I was in Sweden, I kept wondering what my farming grandparents and great- grandparents would have thought of the fact that I was there, teaching at the University. Most of them probably never finished public school, to say nothing of going to the University.

There is much culture in Stockholm. One memorable occasion was when my cousin came to pick us up in a limousine and took us to the Globe Theater to see and hear West End, The Concert with works by Andrew Lloyd Weber and Claude-Michel Schonberg accompanied by the National Symphony Orchestra. The repertoire included selections from Cats, Miss Saigon, Phantom of the Opera, Les Miserables, and Sunset Boulevard. It was in this theater where King Carl XVI Gustaf celebrated his 50th birthday a few weeks later, which we watched on TV in our apartment.

In the summer of 1994, I elected to have surgery to replace a heart valve, which had been damaged by rheumatic fever when I was a young boy. I expected to be fully recovered in time to carry out my plans pertaining to my sabbatical; however, the unexpected happened. Instead of the usual hospital stay of seven or eight days, I ended up being there eleven and a half weeks with five and a half weeks in intensive care on a ventilator. The unforeseen circumstance was that my blood did not coagulate after the surgery and it was necessary to leave my chest open for 2 days until the bleeding stopped.

During this period of two days my chest was invaded by three bacterial infections. Before all was said and done, it nearly cost me my life. I was not expected to live but, because of the grace of God, I survived. I did lose my sabbatical and $20,000, which had been offered as an early retirement incentive, and which I missed by 54 days by having to take forced retirement. (That was a bitter experience in light of the fact that two others received the award on a technicality.)

I informed the University in Stockholm of my situation and they graciously postponed the invitation to teach there for a year and reduced their expectations to one class, which would be taught four days a week. They were most cooperative. The research I had planned to do as part of my sabbatical study was eliminated because of the loss of the sabbatical.

The course I taught was titled "Stress from a Psycho-Biological Perspective." It was a class of "gifted" students, which I thoroughly enjoyed. This experience was a highlight of my career in teaching.

Living in a place for a period of time is much different from being a tourist. While we lived in Stockholm we learned different cultural things, such as the fact that ground beef is beef and ground meat is horse!

G.A.

THE SWEDISH EXCHANGE PROGRAM

NOT AN ORDINARY YEAR

by R. Theodore Smith, Dean of Academic Affairs 1981-1995

Jamestown Community College

I t seemed like it was to be another glorious fall season in Chautauqua County, which was quite ordinary to the local folks. It was not out of the ordinary to have very cool evenings, shorter but bright sunny days, and the usual panorama of color from the turning maple trees painted across all of the hills, in the valleys and around Chautauqua Lake. The blue asters and the goldenrod were ever-present along the roadsides and in the fields again, too, as surely they have been for years and years. The occasional call of a distant pair of loons on Chautauqua Lake could be heard, the yellow school buses were transporting students again, classes were underway at the State University College at Fredonia and at Jamestown Community College, and there was the usual fall automobile sale at the local Chevy dealer. But not everything was the same; there was a change brewing at Jamestown Community College.

It was true then and still is today that Jamestown Community College is the "different one" among the thirty community colleges that belong to the State University of New York. JCC was the first community college in the SUNY system and some say the first brand new community college in the USA after President Truman's major effort to bring access to higher education closer to all Americans. On February 6, 1950, there were no community colleges anywhere in the USA, but the very next day there was one and it was in Jamestown, New York. Out of that pioneering spirit have grown nearly 2400 community colleges in the nation. And in the fall of 1982 a brand new pioneering effort was to emerge again from this innovative community college in Jamestown.

Over the aroma of a cup of fresh coffee and good conversation one fall afternoon, plans were being developed at JCC for a most unusual program to be formulated at a community college. It was certainly true that many colleges and universities throughout the land had a plethora of student exchange programs with other countries, but there were no community colleges in the USA at that time with an existing student exchange program with any of the five Scandinavian countries.

JCC had been sending students and community residents to the West End of London for a two-week experience as part of a theater course for a good many years, as well as students to universities in Spain, South America and Germany, but never did JCC have a formal student exchange with a Scandinavian country.

Into my office one day with proposal in hand walked Professor Gordon Anderson. After the normal greetings and procuring a cup of fresh coffee, he announced that he wanted to discuss an innovative student exchange program between JCC and an educational institution in Sweden.

As we probed deeper into the proposal and discussed what would have to be done at JCC to make the new program possible, a sense of genuine excitement began to build. The basic idea was to enhance the diversity and richness of the JCC educational experience by offering students an opportunity to study in Sweden for a semester. In similar fashion, Swedish students would be able to attend JCC for a semester to broaden their experiences and to enrich the Jamestown campus. It seemed a natural match, since 41% of the population in the Jamestown area at that time was of Swedish heritage.

Because JCC is a community college, we thought that the "community" that supports the college would be very pleased to have a student exchange program with the land of their ancestors with which so many still had contacts. After all, we reasoned, the Swedes of Jamestown had made enormous contributions to the social, cultural, industrial and political climate of the Chautauqua region. There was a Swedish museum in Jamestown, several Swedish social and fraternal clubs, and many of Sweden's diplomats had visited here, the Uppsala Choir had performed here, and even King Carl XVI Gustaf of Sweden had made a recent visit to the community. Prof. Anderson was proposing to enhance this cultural enrichment with one more program, but this time one that involved young people.

What does it take to organize, finance, and implement such a student exchange program? JCC did have some in-house expertise with student programs with other European nations as well as Mexico, but Scandinavia was a new challenge. Neither Prof. Anderson nor I knew at that time what educational institutions in Sweden we might connect with, but we agreed to do some additional research. We talked about the University of Stockholm and the prestigious Uppsala University, but until the research was done, we did not know if they would be interested, perhaps already having too many other existing commitments with American universities, or just how they might react to a proposal from an American community college.

Financing another student exchange program at JCC would have to be addressed, the curricular experiences would have to match so that students would remain on schedule to earn their degrees, and the State University of New York would have to agree to the proposal. Surely, we would also have to have internal support at the college and the community would be asked to lend support for the many other things not mentioned here, but necessary for the success of the program. It was agreed that Prof. Anderson would begin the research on locating an educational institution in Sweden with whom we might articulate, and I, as the JCC Academic Dean, would begin the research on the finances, the curricular issues and traveling to Albany in an effort to win the support of SUNY Central.

The evenings grew colder now as October faded and Thanksgiving was on the horizon. It had been about a month since Anderson and I had met to discuss the project, but we were both very busy doing the necessary research on the feasibility of the new student exchange program. And then one day the phone rang and Anderson said he was ready to recommend a post-secondary educational institution in Jönköping, Sweden, with whom we might initiate an exchange of students. I too announced that my research had borne some fruit and that it was time for some "next steps."

The familiar smile of Gordon Anderson greeted me for our next meeting at my JCC office, and behind the smile was the happiness of a man who had been successful in his first efforts to locate an exchange partner in Sweden. We had guessed correctly that the Swedish universities already had student exchange commitments in the USA and were unable to handle a new program at that time. Anderson had located a Swedish friend who recommended a student exchange between JCC and the Södra Vätterbygdens Folkhögskola (SVF) in Jönköping, Sweden. It was necessary for Prof. Anderson to educate me on the Swedish Folkhögskola because I was unfamiliar with this level of post-secondary education. Once my education on this subject was complete, I too was enthusiastic about the feasibility of an exchange between SVF and JCC.

As luck would have it, the Head Administrator (Rektor) of the Jönköping SVF was visiting the USA that same fall. Arrangements were made to send Prof. Anderson as the college's representative to meet the Swedish educator at a meeting in Oneonta, NY, to discuss the possibilities of an exchange. Anderson was authorized by me to advise the SVF representative that JCC and SUNY had both given their support to a Scandinavian student exchange program. After doing some curricular research on SVF, I authorized Prof. Anderson to offer the point of view that the curricular matches between our two institutions were indeed possible. Still unresolved were the financial commitments, but those too were being worked on inside the college.

18) Program founders Gunnar Hallingberg and Gordon

The Oneonta meeting was very successful[18] and Anderson returned to the campus with an agreement in his pocket! Now we could move forward with vigor to put together the nation's first student exchange program at the community college level. We even thought of writing a feature story for one of the national community college journals, but that would have to wait until all of the pieces were in place.

The days and weeks went by quickly and a great deal of planning work was accomplished. All of the curricular issues were resolved at JCC and SVF.

Prof. Anderson was working in the Swedish community to inform them of the student exchange with Sweden and they were thrilled! Gordon did most of the work in contacting Swedish Organizations and individuals in the Jamestown area by radio, letters and telephone to secure the much needed financial resources to support the project. SUNY offered its support in writing. The second floor office of Prof. Anderson at the

19) The first students in the exchange with SVF

Hultquist Building on campus was abuzz with students making inquiries about whether they might study abroad in Sweden for a semester and have it all count toward the degree program they were enrolled in at JCC. Now we were cooking!

1982 had turned into 1983 and this would be the first year in which JCC students[19] would actually be studying in Sweden in a formal exchange. It was necessary for Prof. Anderson to travel to Jönköping that year to make the final arrangements for the arrival of our first six students to be in the program. That, too, was accomplished in record time and with excellence.

The costs associated with the exchange were worked out with some contributions via private donations to defray part of the costs during those first three years to get the program started. It was grand to see the students departing Jamestown for Toronto to catch a plane to Copenhagen, Denmark. From there our small band of students took the ferry across to Sweden and went by rail to Jönköping to begin their studies. What an achievement this was for Prof. Anderson and for Jamestown Community College.(Note: It should be added that participation in the program was not based solely on grades.)

One of the requirements JCC had for each of the participants was that they purchase a Euro-rail pass so they could travel around Scandinavia and other parts of Europe. This was a great hit and helped our students to experience diversity, altered perceptions and modified attitudes. At the end of the semester, arrangements had been made for the JCC students to have a Baltic Sea experience and this took them to St. Petersburg and Moscow in the USSR. What a bonus this was for our students!

Summer came and went that year, and as the big band sounds from the Casino at Bemus Point faded for another season, students from Sweden were beginning to arrive at the Driftwood residence of Gordon and Geri Anderson to begin the other half of the exchange experience. JCC welcomed half a dozen Swedish students that fall, who enriched our campus and our communities as they were housed in private homes.

And so the pioneering spirit that provided for the beginning of JCC itself had again emerged, this time in the mind of Prof. Gordon Anderson, who dreamed of what might be possible to link the heritage of many local people with the land of their ancestors and who used education to achieve it.

That dream became a reality and many area residents, Swedish-Americans and non-Swedish-Americans alike, have benefited significantly from this valuable experience. As I am sure the reader can appreciate, there is a lot more to this story, but we are all indebted to Gordon Anderson for his insight, dedication, and creative energy in making the Swedish exchange program a success.

Note: Sadly, R. Theodore (Ted) Smith passed away on February 23, 2006 after suffering a heart attack

SIGNIFICANT PORTRAITS

Lynne Weber

`ynne Weber is secretary for the Division of Social Sciences at Jamestown Community College. She started as a student secretary in the same year as I began at JCC, 1967, and continued in that role until 1969. As I remember, she was not a particularly good typist in the very beginning; but in 1970 she was offered the job of secretary and was on probation for a few months before it was finalized. She more or less stayed with the division, but did work in the administrative offices at times. But she liked the division better. By this time we were in the new building, Hultquist Learning Center (LISS). She had become an excellent typist and secretary and she shared the typing with one other secretary. They typed tests, letters and schedules.

When I became division chairman of Behavioral Sciences, which included psychology, sociology, anthropology and philosophy, I had more contact with Lynne. Also, the rule was, at that time, that she could do other personal work if her college work was done. She also said she would rather be busy than to just sit there, so she assumed the work of the other secretary, who by that time had left the division.

20) Lynne Weber

Lynne did a lot of personal typing for me, on her own time, when I was in county government. She got to know my mind so well I swear she could read it! On tests and letters she always corrected my mistakes. When I retired from the college, I felt like I had lost my right arm.

Lynne is a great gal!

G.A.

SIGNIFICANT PORTRAITS

Harry Bridges

H enry (Harry) Bridges was a psychology professor, a dean, and more at Jamestown Community College, where, as division chairperson in the psychology department, he hired me to teach in 1967. From the time I met him, he was an important mentor for me and he also became a close friend to both my wife and me.

21) Henry Jed Bridges

He was a strong believer in women's strengths. Therefore he developed a unique program at the College, called "Potential of Women," which allowed homemakers and working women to further their education. In fact, my wife, Geri, enrolled in the program shortly after it began in the late 1960s. After her experience there, she went into business with our "Northshore Farmhouse—Country Delectables and Other Happy Things" mail-order enterprise.

"The direction [Harry Bridges] gave me, and all of us really," Geri says, "was to be whatever you wanted to be. Just because you are a woman and a mother, you don't have to sit home . . . . He really inspired all of his students to reach out for something."

For me, the encouragement and support I got from Harry was phenomenal. He encouraged me in my run for the county legislature, and in carrying out my duties when I was there. And he supported me in working out logistics when I decided to return to the university to work towards getting a Ph.D.

When he died—far too soon—in 1990, I missed him very much, and still do.

G.A.

SIGNIFICANT PORTRAITS

John Collins

M y best friend, and closest colleague, throughout my more than
30 years of teaching at Jamestown
Community College was Dr. John
Collins, who taught anthropology.

22) John Collins

He was an excellent teacher, and one
who therefore was a constant inspiration to
me. He won numerous awards, including the
National Institute for Staff and Organizational
Development Award for Excellence in
Teaching, the JCC Faculty Award for
Excellence in Teaching, and the New York
State Chancellor's Award for Excellence in
Teaching. He was the first faculty member to
deliver the keynote address at commence-
ment. He was a driving force to form the college's honor society, and was the author of several books on anthropology and Native Americans.

Just by accident John and I discovered that we used similar approaches
to our teaching. We both used Carole Burnett's technique of warming up the
audience before we started to teach and we found that was an effective way
to reach our students. It was both fun and funny when we compared notes
and found we were both doing the same thing.

When John died prematurely at age 60 of a heart attack, it hit me hard. I
had been depending on him to continue to be my friend forever. When his
wife asked me to handle the funeral, it was one of the most difficult things
I've ever had to do. Somehow, though, I was both able to give comfort to the
other mourners and to find it for myself as I paid tribute to my dear, dear
friend.

G.A.

PHOTO GALLERY-3

1) Our home on Driftwood in 1963

2) The view from our home

3) Library at JCC, 1967

4) Gordon with students after psychology class

5) Typical student housing at Claremont Graduate School

6) Debra Lawson checks on her rat experiment

7) City Hall, Lidköping Sweden

10) SVF Cafeteria

12) The beautiful Uppsala Cathedral

PHOTO GALLERY-3

13) Viking Burial Mounds in Old Uppsala

14) Forsmark, a repository for spent atomic fuel

16) A sample of the art found in each underground station

17) The one block complex housing Immanuel Church in Stockholm, Sweden

PART 2

THE REVOLUTION BEGINS

CHAPTER FOUR

BUMPY ROAD AHEAD: THE DRIFTWOOD STORY

By the time Gordon Anderson and his family (wife Geri and young son Daniel) returned to Chautauqua County and moved into the house they had bought, and still live in, on Driftwood Road in Bemus Point, their future seemed settled on a course involving teaching and weekend preaching (for Gordon), and lake-living—right back where they wanted to be.

"*To arms! To arms the bulldozers are coming!*"

1) A cartoon sent to me by a friend

Shortly after their return, their second son, David, was born in WCA Hospital in Jamestown, on September 28, 1963.

Then, one night in 1965 Gordon's dad called him and said: "I saw a map today of the route of the new expressway and I noticed that your house is in the median strip." Gordon laughed and said, "You're kidding."

"I got hold of a map," he said, "and our house, lo and behold[1], was in the median strip. So I went up and down all the roads—it's just a need I have, I guess, to kind of organize things or start things or get things accomplished. I went to some houses and people said 'Oh, good! Then we'll get rid of the house and get rid of the mortgage.' Other people said, 'I don't believe you' and slammed the door in my face. Even one of my neighbors did that. But I got two guys across the road to help me—one was Jean Creager, a traveling salesman for Marlin Rockwell, and the other was John Rotsko, who was the superintendent of Hope's Windows and he was an engineer."

The real Driftwood Campaign (a code phrase for the effort to realign the Southern Tier Expressway from Strunk Road to Westman Road in Ellery Township) began sometime in 1965 with a letter to homeowners advising them that New York State Department of Public Works surveyors might be coming onto their property to conduct surveys in connection with the routing of the Southern Tier Expressway.

The letter said "Our engineers, surveyors and workmen are instructed to be courteous and friendly and careful to avoid causing damage in performing their work . . . We earnestly ask your friendly cooperation now, and as this project may continue to develop and affect you."

It also invited letter recipients to contact or visit the DPW Buffalo office "any time you wish to know more about this project."

Then Gordon Anderson received a letter dated October 29, 1965 in response to his inquiry, stating:

"An expressway will be built between Bemus Point and Jamestown generally parallel to the existing Route 17" (now Route 430). The letter discussed the possibility of a bridge over Chautauqua Lake, concluding that "irregardless [sic] of the feasibility of the Bemus Point Bridge, an expressway will be built on your side of the lake." And the letter further advised that a public hearing on the expressway project would be held "sometime in the month of November," and that Gordon and other residents would be notified when the date was set.

The clincher was this chilling notice: "The preliminary location plans of the expressway in your area does [sic] indicate that your home might fall into the proposed right-of-way. But it must be stressed that these plans are very preliminary in nature and are subject to change during the course of design. In your specific location where there is considerable high value development and also difficult topographical features this is especially true."

Thus, even in this preliminary stage, the state DPW was aware of the conditions on which the Driftwood area residents were to base their case— the high value both as real estate and as tax base of the homes that were threatened, and the fact that a highway could be routed differently through and in spite of "difficult topographical features."

By this time the Driftwood residents, led by Gordon and his co-organizers, were determined to try to save their homes. Initially, the DPW thought the residents' motivation was to get more money for their properties. On the contrary, these Driftwood citizens did not want to sell at all.

In a letter to all the residents involved, dated November 4, 1965, Gordon informed them that the "white cross markers" which had recently appeared along their roads meant that the projected route of the expressway would go between those crosses, that their homes might be threatened, and that "we are organizing opposition." He suggested that residents on each road (Driftwood Road, Dutch Hollow Road, and Belleview Road) get up a petition for changing the route, that they attend the upcoming hearing, and that anyone who wanted further information could call him.

In the meantime Gordon alerted all elected representatives from the area about the expressway route problem and asked for their help. These included State Assemblymen Jess Present and A. Bruce Manley, State Senator James F. Hastings, U.S. Congressman Charles E. Goodell, and Town of Ellery Supervisor Richard Evans. To their credit, every one of these officials supported the Driftwood residents' cause and lent support to their effort to enlist Governor Nelson Rockefeller in working for a route change.

The group hired a lawyer, Sherwood Cadwell of Jamestown, whose duties would include attending the public hearings and other meetings with DPW officials.

By February 12, 1966, Gordon was able to write to the involved residents that the DPW had agreed to do another survey for an alternate route, but that it could not be done until the weather cleared.

"In effect," Anderson's letter said, "they said that they don't care where the highway goes, and if we care, they will try to comply with our wishes."

Up to this time the effort to achieve a re-routing had accrued, the letter said, $146.84 in expenses (most of that lawyer's fees) and the residents were asked to contribute their share of $12.23.

The next year or so produced a hornet's nest of developments. A new survey revealed that an alternate route, maintaining a 200-foot median strip, through less valuable scrubland higher on Driftwood Hill, would indeed be possible, but very expensive. Yet the DPW engineers persisted in arguing, falsely as it proved, that the first plan—the DPW original route—should still be pursued. John Rotsko and a hired engineer, Francis Jenkins from JCC, proceeded to figure "cut and fill" to see how much dirt needed to be moved—a large part of the cost of building a highway.

" I was also interested," Gordon said, "in studying the 200 foot median strip requirements. The late Art Briggs flew me down along the area of the Kinzua overflow. Just beyond this area the lanes came much closer together. Later, John Rotsko and I went by car and measured the width of the median strip, using the stakes the state had pounded in. We found it to be only 38 feet, which is in violation of their own book, *A Policy on Geometric Design of Rural Highways, 1965: American Association of State Highway Officials*, which states that 40 feet is the minimum. I don't know for sure, but I wonder if 38 feet was adopted because it was in Indian Territory."

By this time, Gordon said, "We had been turned down eight times, and the last time we were turned down everyone said it's no use trying anymore if we can't get them to compromise. But, me being me, I couldn't leave it alone. I decided I'd keep working at it and Jean and John said, 'If you want to work on it go ahead, we've given up.' I got a huge map from the DPW in Buffalo and I spread it out on the living room floor and "tweaked" it a little. The alternate route was to involve the section from Strunk Road up to Westman Road, but now I modified it a little more.

"I knew they had too much dirt left over, so I drew a line that went through a huge ravine where they had plenty of space to push the dirt and they didn't have to haul it a long distance. Also I knew the politics of it by that time—who was in favor and who wasn't. My modified line was drawn in such a way that we saved 14 houses and we didn't take anyone else's house—it was all through scrubland. Finally, we got a hearing in the Governor's office in Albany. Because of the efforts of Senator Hastings and the Governor's office, we were energized one more time.

"And so we took the modified line that I had drawn and the figures on cut and fill. The state itself had not lied to us, but their consultants, Erdman and Anthony, had tried to trick us many times, as the *Post-Journal* article says. (September 11, 1974) We did get a hearing and J. Burch McMorran, who was the Superintendent of Public Works for the entire state, sat right beside me and I started to read to him the deceiving data that the state consultants had presented to us and, through that, we had learned valuable information on how much it costs to move dirt. So we used their own figures against them. I continued reading this indictment and then presented our final route which I had redrawn and said that we would save at least a half million dollars, which was a big chunk of money in 1966. Also the route would be shorter, and therefore user costs would be less.

"We discussed the median strip," Anderson said, "and told them it did not need to be 200 feet, that their book said 40 feet. Then I brought up the 38 foot discovery. They said, 'We don't build them that way anymore. That is an old project.' I said, it can't be too old, you haven't even poured the concrete yet!"

"[Mr. McMorran] leaned over to me and said, 'Young man, do you have a copy of what you're reading? I want to check that out.' I think his eyes were really opened. I said, 'I think I can find a copy' and, of course, I had a whole bunch of copies in my briefcase. So I gave him a copy.

"They never formally told us in writing that they would change the highway. They tried to mislead us in a lot of different ways, but finally I got a phone call in my classroom at Jamestown High School and was told the high-way is going to be moved approximately to your plan and I was really excited over that. I've heard since then that we are the only group in the history of the state that figured their own route and got it adopted by the DOT. And I'm very proud of that. And it wasn't just my effort, it was my effort at the end, maybe, but it was largely the efforts of these other guys who worked with me, Jean, John, Gerald Hunt and Fran Jenkins, plus Jess Present, Bruce Manley and Charles Goodell. There were some others, too. Sam Valone, who was a realtor, figured out how much would be lost if the houses were removed from the tax rolls and things like that. So we had a lot of information. It took us almost two years to get the highway alignment changed.

We did not wage this fight emotionally. We didn't say that we're going to sit on our porches with a shotgun and if you come and try to build a highway here we're going to shoot you. We tried to use good judgment and intelligence."

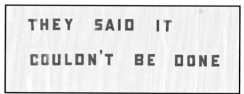

2) Our table banner

On July 24, 1967—almost exactly two years since the first notice from the DPW—the Driftwood group held a celebration dinner at the Hare 'N' Hounds restaurant in Bemus Point, complete with a banner over the head table which read "THEY SAID IT COULDN'T BE DONE"[2]. They invited all the people who had played a part in moving the effort towards its successful conclusion, among them Congressman Charles Goodell. In his letter of response[3], sending regrets that because of responsibilities in Washington he and Mrs. Goodell could not attend, Goodell added a handwritten note:

"You should be congratulated on a superb job of winning an unusual victory over bureaucracy!" he wrote.

It was not until seven years later that the Driftwood group went public with their full story and the *Jamestown Post-Journal* ran a feature story remembering the Driftwood Campaign and its success. And then it published an editorial comment:

"The story of how the Driftwood Road residents succeeded in saving their neighborhood by presenting alternatives to the expressway's path remains a pertinent example for all . . . . Criticism may be helpful and valid but good citizenship is exemplified by those who take the time to analyze the situation and suggest concrete proposals for change or compromise. It isn't always easy but honest effort works wonders . . . Perhaps the record book would show more favorable statistics in such matters if more of us followed up our convictions with determination and hard work."

Following up convictions with determination and hard work is vintage Gordon Anderson. Thanks to him and his citizen fellows, the Southern Tier Expressway is now finished through a beautiful section of western New York and into Pennsylvania. It is a road which cost much less to build and is shorter than it might otherwise have been resulting in lower costs to use it. It provides beautiful lake vistas and a rest stop for travelers, overlooking Chautauqua Lake, has not ruined a neighborhood, and has preserved on the tax rolls a dozen high-value properties, plus other homes which have since been built on the prime hillside area it skirts.

And all because Gordon Anderson and his neighbors responded to the threat against their homes and the view of the lake they loved. It seems almost providential that Gordon returned from California just in time to realign the route of the Southern Tier Expressway, now U.S. Highway I-86.

An interesting anecdote to this story is that the bulldozers found evidence of an Indian village close to Townline Road as they approached from Strunk Road. Also in the vicinity is a small bird sanctuary so the DOT moved the highway project to the North to avoid it.

Because of the very difficult and hilly terrain between Dutch Hollow Road and Driftwood Road – with a ravine, heavy brushy growth and a creek bed to deal with – the trail blazing bulldozer operator found himself in a precarious and vulnerable position. He was not sure if he would come to a sudden drop -off or suddenly go "head over heels". Fortunately he got to the bottom of the ravine without incident and safely made his way up the hill to Driftwood road. His was a lonely and tense job, indeed. (See picture #4 which follows.)

CHARLES E. GOODELL
HOUSE OF REPRESENTATIVES
WASHINGTON, D. C.

July 17, 1967

Mrs. Gordon E. Anderson
Driftwood - Box 282
Bemus Point, New York

Dear Mrs. Anderson:

Thank you so much for your cordial invitation to be the dinner guests of the Driftwood residents at the Hare 'N' Hounds in Bemus Point on the evening of Monday, July 24th.

Mrs. Goodell and I wish we could be there to join with you in celebrating the recent victory in the Route 17 battle. Unfortunately, my responsibilities in connection with an important all-day meeting of the Republican Coordinating Committee in Washington on that date will prevent us from being with you.

Please express our personal greetings and warm best wishes to all those who gather together on this happy occasion. We appreciate your thinking of us and you can be sure we will be thinking of you.

With kindest regards, I am

Very truly yours,

Charlie Goodell

Charles E. Goodell

You should be congratulated on a superb job of winning an unusual victory over adversary!

3) The letter from our Congressman

67

PHOTO GALLERY- 4

4) Looking up a steep hill from a deep valley between between Dutch Hollow and Driftwood

5) An early 20th century split rail fence, waiting to be disturbed by progress

6) Gordon checking out the first run through by a Groves construction dozer

7) Gordon follows the progress

8) Big equipment moves in to cover a culvert(white area, lower right corner

9)

10)

11)

12)

13)

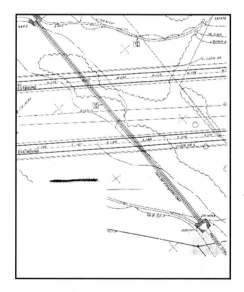

14) 2 diagonal sluice-ways under the East and West bound lanes at Driftwood. The sluice pipes are 750' long, 54" diameter

15) Map showing the evolution of the final expressway route

CHAPTER FIVE

I EMBARK ON A POLITICAL CAREER

I n 1971, after a successful summer as manager of the North Shore Inn at Chautauqua in its final season, Gordon Anderson found himself with extra money for perhaps the first time in his life. Moreover, reflecting on the experience gained through the "Driftwood Campaign," where Gordon and his neighbors succeeded in changing the route of the Southern Tier Expressway so it wouldn't threaten their homes and property, he got the idea of running for public office. His reasons were that he had the opportunity, he felt he had the skills, and, as a caring citizen, he even had the responsibility to work in some way for the public good.

"This was not something I had ever planned on doing, and I don't think that God called me to do it, but I did feel a direction to do it as an American and to take my turn, as it were."

Therefore, in the summer of 1971, he teamed up[1] with Arden Johnson, who was running, for the first time, for the post of Ellery Town Supervisor, and Craig Miller, first-time candidate for Ellery Councilman, to circulate petitions seeking the Republican nomination on the 1971 election ballot. The office that Gordon sought was to represent District Five (the towns of Ellery and Gerry) in the first Chautauqua County Legislature. (Prior to this time the County had been under the management of a Board of Supervisors comprising all the town supervisors in the County. Now, new organization[2] would change the scene so that there would be both town supervisors and county legislators.)

In Gordon's case, he faced a seemingly stiff September primary for the Republican nomination against three other men[3]: C. Elmer Carlson, the incumbent Gerry supervisor; John L. Goodell, an attorney; and John C. Cheney, a well-known farmer. Gordon won the nomination easily. His votes totaled 279, as against 210 for Cheney, 203 for Goodell and 149 for Carlson.

This primary and the general election, which followed in November, had several interesting aspects, some making history. As previously noted, the elections would result in a county legislature-governance structure for the first time in the county's history. Secondly, it would be the first time 18-year-olds (and 19- and 20-year-olds, obviously) would be eligible to vote in New York State. According to the Jamestown Post-Journal, approximately 5,000 young people had been registered to vote by the time of the general election.

4) Gordon as chairman, 1978

A third history-making situation was that it would be the first time both a father and son ran for legislative seats, interestingly, in different districts and in opposing parties: Elliott H. Kidder (father) as a Republican, and Rolland E. Kidder (son) as a Democrat.

Finally, whether it was a first or not, it was extraordinary: Attorney John Goodell wrote a letter to the Post-Journal less than a week after the primary election praising his successful opponent, Gordon Anderson, as follows: "I am well-satisfied with the candidate who won. I first became acquainted with [him] during this campaign. He is intelligent and capable and in my opinion will make an excellent county legislator. I would urge that Republicans and Democrats vote for him; he is the kind of person we need in politics today."

Thus, even before assuming office, Gordon Anderson was launched as a distinctive and unusual politician. And again, in the November general election he won easily, defeating his Democratic opponent, Ralph H. Goold, Jr., by 1372 votes to 732. However, the legislature he was elected to was to be controlled by Democrats, with 15 seats to the Republicans' 10. One of the Democrats was Joseph Gerace, elected as one of two legislators representing District 7 (Busti and Harmony). Gerace would figure in the legislative history of Gordon Anderson in many ways—as an often vigorous and determined political opponent, as county executive (later) versus Anderson as legislature chairman[4], as willing compromiser/coworker in working to achieve effective county government, and as respected and respectful friend.

From the beginning, Gordon Anderson served his constituency and the county he lived in with distinction. Unlike one legislator from another district (a friend of Gordon's) who was characterized by a constituent as a do-nothing who wanted to "do nothing more than to stand behind his grocery counter and cut cheese," Gordon was tireless. He responded to needs and requests from his district constituents in almost every case, often with successful action, always with at least feedback when he was not successful. He also initiated action where he saw a problem or a need.

"While I was a legislator," he said, "I tried to be as active as I could. During my four terms I looked into such things as whether Chautauqua County needed more nursing homes. I also proposed a Chautauqua

Watershed District (to raise funds to clean up the lake), which I don't think had been proposed before, and for that I was told by my colleagues in the legislature that I was committing political suicide. I got at least one nasty letter and a couple of supportive letters, but I could not sell it because it would involve a small tax. (As you got closer to the lake, land owners would pay more.) But it didn't go through. No one likes to raise taxes. It was a very small raise but nevertheless I got a lot of flak."

Interestingly though in the early 2000s, a Chautauqua Lake Watershed District is once again being advocated. Efforts are proceeding to get the New York state legislature to pass a home-rule law, which would enable Chautauqua County to establish a lake-control district responsible for maintaining the quality and standards of Chautauqua Lake. A small tax to be imposed on property would fund the effort, which would then do what is necessary to keep the lake clean, attractive and usable for all the many activities associated with it.

That Gordon Anderson took the leadership in trying to get such a solution as long ago as the mid-1970s illustrates the influence he had—and could have had—if opposition to imposing another tax had not carried the day nearly 30 years ago. The tax would be, in one expert's opinion, probably not more than five cents per thousand dollar assessment at the start. The benefit to the county, to its residents, its economy, and its quality of life, however, would be large—as Gordon perceived when he proposed such a district years ago. And he is still "in the saddle," so to speak. Following an interpretative news feature on the reasons for establishing a lake district that appeared in the *Post-Journal* on February 2, 2003 (written by Sue Weaver), Gordon sent a letter to the P-J editor, which appeared in the Feb. 23 issue under the headline "Lake Stewardship." In part, it read:

"As a boy, I remember seeing raw sewage float by as I was swimming. In a forthcoming book on Chautauqua Lake, I will describe the huge efforts by many people to get the lake sewered. The sewer systems helped considerably in cleaning the lake by eliminating the raw sewage.

"In the mid-1970s, I introduced a resolution in the County Legislature to create a watershed maintenance district to help fund the cleaning up of Lake Chautauqua. There were public hearings, but it was not readily supported by the media and it died in committee because it contained a very modest tax, 5 cents per $1,000 at the farthest point from the lake and slightly increasing as it moved closer to the lake . . . .I would be glad to help [with a workable plan] to the extent that I am able . . . .I encourage you, Sue, and others, to get on with it!"

As Gordon Anderson would say, "Me being me," he's still working to make a difference for Chautauqua County.

After being first elected to the fledgling county legislature in 1971, Gordon was a candidate for re-election three more times[5,6,7], in 1973, 1975, and 1977. Each time he won easily. In the 1973 election he got 73% of the vote over his opponent Gordon Nordlund; in 1975 he got 63% over opponent Tom Shagla. And in 1977, he won over Jonathan Hamilton by a similar margin.

RE-ELECT

Gordon E.

ANDERSON

COUNTY LEGISLATOR
Ellery & Gerry

7) Campaign Poster

After a long battle over establishing sewers around much of the lake, he decided not to run for re-election in 1979. More to the point, though, he was heavily involved in his teaching and related activities (an exchange program between Jamestown Community College and Södra Vätterbygdens Folkhögskola in Sweden, for instance), and, as he said, "he had other mountains to climb."

As a legislator, beginning in 1972, Gordon actively pursued solutions for many different issues. His constituents, as has already been indicated, brought some, to his attention. These included medical/health problems in the county, the need for more adequate nursing-home care, the condition of county roads, and—perennially—the quality of the water of Lake Chautauqua.

For instance, an ongoing problem with the route of Highway 60 through Gerry, where there were many accidents, was a frequent Gordon Anderson concern. He wrote often to state legislators, Department of Transportation officials, and local highway supervisors in an attempt to have the route corrected for greater safety. It took far longer than he or anyone else wanted, but there is now a clearly visible turn, marked by a four-way stop, which rectified the problem.

In another case, early in the 1970s, Gordon was part of an investigation to determine whether there was a need for more nursing home space in the county for the care of elderly and disabled citizens, including the possibility of building a County Infirmary in the south county (in addition to one in the town of Dunkirk). A meeting under legislature auspices was held in Mayville, with nursing home owners and supervisors and other health-care professionals in attendance. As a result of this meeting and the effort behind it, Gordon says, "I think it served to highlight the problem and from then on more homes were built; they [owners and supervisors] took action privately or on their own, and so I think the effort did have a good effect."

A third program initiated in the county during those years was for recruiting physicians to serve the most rural areas of the county. Medical students were granted $5000 in return for a promise to practice in the county after graduation. As a result at least three physicians established practices in rural communities during the mid-1970s. Other efforts went toward improving the attention to and care of mental health issues in the county.

In addition, for a county legislator in Gordon's time (and still today), there was responsibility to serve on legislative committees (agencies, central services, compensation insurance, finance, judicial, legislative, personnel, public safety, public works, and social services), which met at least once a month. There was at least one monthly full-legislature meeting. There was the responsibility to attend necessary public hearings on subjects involved in the committee agendas. There were frequent political, social or public-minded events where the legislators were expected to make an appearance. And the legislators, for the most part, held full-time jobs as well, in Gordon's case, as professor of psychology at Jamestown Community College.

This brings up two matters: what about party affiliation and the responsibilities thereto, and what about workload?

Gordon has interesting answers to both questions:

"Of course I ran with a party affiliation[8] and as a result was a member of either the minority party or the majority in the legislature itself. There were always certain things on which I voted with the party—like naming the official newspaper, for instance. The Republicans usually named the *Jamestown Post-Journal*; the Democrats, usually the Dunkirk *Observer*.

"But on many issues I was my own man and I always said my conscience came first and my party came second. And one time I came up there [Mayville] and the election commissioner for the Republicans said, 'Now you're all going to vote yes on this thing today.' And I said, 'I'm not.' And he said,' 'Well, we won't support you then.' 'And I said, 'Well, you didn't support me before, so . . . '

"I never accepted any money from the party, ever. I got $85 one time and I returned it because I didn't want to feel that I was beholden to anyone. And I tried to do what I thought was best for the people and I think that's the best politics.

"But I got a certain amount of criticism about that. I was told I was 'too honest to be in politics.' What an indictment that is!"

As for workload, Gordon's view is this: "Being in the legislature is as time-consuming as you let it be, especially if you're in the majority."

Yet for Gordon, because he is the kind of person he is, his workload was always heavy. Right from the beginning, because of circumstances, he was heavily involved in the important issue of reapportionment. When he was first elected, the changing government meant that instead of having a legislature composed of all the county supervisors, there would be a governing body composed of representatives from districts comprising, in some cases, more than one town and, in others, several wards or districts within the county's two cities, Jamestown and Dunkirk.

Following the national census of 1970, Justice Charles J. Gaughan of the Erie County Supreme Court had issued an order for a temporary legislature in Chautauqua County, under the state's Municipal Home Rule Law, comprised of 25 members representing 12 districts. But there was also a directive to reapportion the districts to meet a one-person, one-vote standard. In the new legislature to which Gordon Anderson was elected, a reapportionment committee was appointed, with Robert Kron, Democrat, as chair, and Gordon was a member. Before long a new plan emerged, for a 23-member legislature, with district boundaries redrawn, and it was dubbed the "Democrat plan."

Although his own district of Ellery and Gerry was left intact, other districts would have what Gordon termed "curious arrangements," such as throwing all of the town of West Ellicott in with Jamestown Wards 4, 5, 6 and 7, to elect four legislative members at large; and throwing the Village of Celeron in with Jamestown Wards 1, 2, and 3, electing three legislative members at large. Thus, Gordon said, "it appears West Ellicott and the Village of Celeron will be disemboweled by Jamestown politics," producing conflicts of interest and violating the one-person, one-vote standard.

Gordon was not the only one who opposed the 23-member plan. There are letters in his records from others who were vigorous in their opposition, especially one vocal and determined West Ellicott resident, Ernest Leet, who was well-known in the county as an attorney and citizen activist.

However, Gordon was on the scene as legislator and committee member, and he had also published opinion articles opposing the plan in the local papers. A referendum was held—at the instigation of County Republicans—in November 1973, and the 23-legislator plan was soundly defeated.

In the wake of the defeat, Joseph Gerace, who was still at that point legislature chairperson (he had been elected to be the first County Executive in that same November election), called a meeting with Reapportionment Committee chairperson Robert Kron and vocal opponent Gordon Anderson to try to work out an agreement on districts and their representation.

"I was the one who was doing the hollering," Gordon said, "so Joe asked me, 'Well, O.K., what do you think the number should be?' I said '25.' 'Well, O.K.,' he said, 'let's go with 25.'"

"A judge must have approved it," Gordon says, "but at any rate that's the solution that was reached." And it's been a 25-person legislature ever since, though interestingly, at the time of this writing, there is another movement afoot to cut the legislature membership to 17, for reasons of economy in a time of very tight budgeting.

In the six years remaining of Gordon's term in the legislature, he was involved in several more important issues affecting the quality of life in Chautauqua County, among them whether or not to build a bridge over Lake Chautauqua to connect the Southern Tier Expressway, whether to build and how to manage sewer districts around the lake to deal with the problem of waste and pollution of the lake, and whether to establish a landfill for solid waste disposal and where to locate it. In addition, in his last term (1978-79), he would be elected Chairperson of the Legislature.

How he dealt with these issues and responsibilities continued to make a difference for the people of Chautauqua County, as the story to be told in the next chapters will show.[9, 10, 11]

1) Anderson, Johnson &
Miller.

2) Legislative Districts

3) Hello letter

5) Election Sign

6) 1973 Candidates

8) The ballot for November 1975

9) Gordon with student interns and
County Executive Gerace

10) Chautaqua County Court House

11) Gerace office Building and Holland Land Company
Vault built where records of the Land company were
kept until the late 1800s

CHAPTER SIX

GETTING ACROSS, OR AROUND, THE LAKE

During his first term in office as a county legislator Gordon Anderson and the rest of the citizens of Chautauqua County, found themselves confronting an issue that was to divide public opinion as few other issues ever did, and that would cause a delay in the solution for years, at a tremendous cost to the county, the state, and the federal government as well.

The issue was the proposed bridge over Chautauqua Lake at, or near, the "narrows" between Bemus Point on the east and Stow on the west. The bridge would serve two purposes: it would be what many considered the best connection between the eastern and western sections of the Southern Tier Expressway which had been being progressively built through the southern part of New York State for more than a decade. Eventually the expressway would become part of the highway network, spider-webbing the entire United States from east to west and north to south. It took an entire decade for the road to be completed through the short section (approximately 30 miles) from the Jamestown exit on the east, across the lake, and up to the state's border with Pennsylvania. It took still more years to build another unfinished section through Salamanca (also a contested segment) and the Pennsylvania section, only a few miles long, to complete the link with the cross-nation superhighway that is Interstate 90. Finally, at the date of this writing, the Southern Tier Expressway, now renamed Interstate 86, is complete, although there is still a long section on the eastern end which has not yet been renumbered from NY 17 to I 86.

An oddity, in 1972, was that the state had already started to build an expressway section on the other side of the lake. Legislator Joseph Lepkowski, who represented a district west of the lake near the Pennsylvania border, brought to the attention of the other legislators that construction crews were working in the Sherman area and, Gordon remembers, in the French Creek area.

"The idea of the DOT, I think," Gordon says, "was to force the building of the bridge. Some areas were actually bulldozed for four lanes, but eventually only two lanes were paved and the other lanes just left in rough bulldozing. Once the bridge was built, this maneuver proved to be a tragic mistake, for many drivers forgot the road was only two lanes, not four, and many were killed. Sheriff Joseph Gerace, Jr., has said the number, according to his records, was 24."

Getting from one side of Lake Chautauqua to the other had been a concern of county residents since 1811, with licensing of the first ferry to travel the Bemus Point-to-Stow narrows. The ferry has operated continuously[1,2] in season (spring to late fall) since that date. However, by the time of Gordon Anderson's tenure in the legislature, and in part connected with the plans for the lake bridge, being able to keep the ferry in operation had become another problem for the legislature to deal with, and for Gordon himself because, as it happened, one half of both the ferry route and the bridge over the lake were in the legislative district he represented. (The other half was in North Harmony).

During the century and a half between the ferry's maiden voyage and the planned building of the lake bridge, Chautauqua County residents, and visitors and tourists who came to enjoy the activities the lake provided, had several choices: If they were coming down from the north, northeast or northwest, they could either drive around the lake, take the ferry across in season (and, in earlier years, one of a couple of other ferries), or simply plan to stay for a particular day's excursion on one side of the lake or the other. In earlier years, during the winter, some drove across the ice and a few perished because the ice was thin because of currents from the upper to the lower lake.

If people were coming from Jamestown and other points southeast or southwest, they had the same choices. And for a period from 1904 to 1926, they could take a train up or down one side or the other. In other words, Lake Chautauqua has always been central to the quality of life in the county and both residents and visitors used it in many ways. So a quick way across the lake certainly had its appeal.

In 1972, with plans underway for a bridge over the lake, Gordon Anderson found himself among those who did not want a bridge built over what was "their" lake. They opposed the bridge both on aesthetic grounds (it would simply spoil the beauty they loved) and environmentally (although Gordon was not a member of the environmentalist group which stopped the bridge). Many believed that the bridge would surely mean more pollution of the lake, from run-off, silt and other things, plus it might have other effects no one could anticipate.

Newly elected to the County Legislature, Gordon decided to poll his constituents on the subject of the bridge. He sent out questionnaires to 450 residents of his district; and got 170 returns. Of those who responded, the majority opposed the bridge. In addition, Gordon knew of other objections connected with the bridge plans and the highway route. Together with Theodore Smith, who represented a Jamestown district, he introduced a resolution asking that the Department of Transportation (DOT) hold a public meeting so residents could learn exactly what was in the plans, and asking that the DOT also conduct an in-depth study of alternate routes that would go south to

3) Cutting off the pilings

circumvent Chautauqua Lake and meet state and federal requirements. This resolution was adopted on May 12, 1972.

Later in the year several legislators introduced a resolution to endorse the completion of the bridge project. Citing a rising tide of opposition to the bridge (for instance, 2300 responses to a newspaper ad on the question), Gordon once again took the lead in suggesting that the resolution be tabled for two months in order to investigate further what the people really wanted. In the discussion following the successful vote to table, Legislator Lepkowski cited information obtained from an Erie, PA newspaper and a letter from Planning Director John Luensman asserting that Pennsylvania would begin construction of their portion of the highway in 1975. This would refute claims that the portion of the highway including the bridge would be a road "going to nowhere."

When the resolution to support completion of the highway was taken off the table at the November 8, 1972 meeting, Gordon, agreeing with his co-sponsor Ted Smith that the conditions they had been concerned about had been satisfactorily addressed, said:

"As I've stated before, I believe the majority of the people in my district have been opposed to this. However, some of the objections have been satisfied. I am glad the ecological report and considerations have been read into the record. I think that makes many of us feel more comfortable. There is one aspect, however, that I have not been satisfied with, and that is a description really of what it is going to look like and what can be done to make this as attractive as possible . . . .I would like more information on the aesthetics: Are there going to be plantings along the approaches? What's this going to look like? What color is the bridge going to be? These are things we have a right to know because we are living here and have to look at it."

When the resolution was re-introduced he voted, he said, "reluctantly" for the resolution, which passed unanimously.

However, in 1974, as building the bridge and completing the highway were moving slowly forward, a group of environmentalists sought an injunction against proceeding with the bridge. They were objecting to it mainly on

4) The Watson mansion was razed to make way for the West end of the bridge, leaving only the servants quarters standing

the grounds that an environmental impact study (EIS), required by federal law, had not been done. Buffalo Federal Judge Robert Curtin, who had jurisdiction, granted the injunction to stop work on the bridge until such a study was completed. At this point the pilings for the bridge[3] had to be cut off and the land on both sides seeded and returned to normal. That cost the state $6 million, all of it unrecoverable. Following this injunction, four years would elapse before work on the bridge resumed.

In the meantime, the Chautauqua County Legislature kept a hand in. Periodic resolutions in support of resuming bridge construction were adopted. In 1975, to test the legislature, Ted Smith and Gordon Anderson cosponsored a resolution against the bridge. It was voted down by 23 no votes, with only 2 yeas. Then Gordon sent out another questionnaire to his constituents. Respondents to this survey still opposed the bridge: 65% in Ellery and 73% in Gerry (with 34% and 24% in favor, respectively).

With things just hanging in the balance, however, with nothing going forward, with the expressway in limbo and with inconvenience for local residents—and visitors—ever-present, people wanted a solution.

In 1977, Gordon issued still a third survey of his constituents on the question of the bridge. This time, as a July 1977 editorial from station WJTN in Jamestown, put it, "He found 71 percent of the 424 persons who answered his questionnaire want work on the bridge resumed . . . .While the future of the bridge should hardly be based on a popularity contest, it is significant that residents of Mr. Anderson's district—the one where the bridge will be located—are clearly in favor of it . . . .If the environmental impact report—required by the court action brought against the bridge—shows no serious problem, then let's get the bridge built."

Finally, in 1978, things began to move[4]. In February, the Federal Department of Transportation gave its approval to the Environmental Impact Statement, which had been required under the injunction imposed by Judge Curtin in 1974. The report on this was given by District Superintendent Donald Ketchum. One legislator with poor hearing kept asking questions of "Mr. Ketchup," as he called him.

Meanwhile, the lawyer for the people who had sought the injunction continued to fight resumption of bridge construction. In May 1978 Judge Curtin heard arguments from both sides, and on May 5, he lifted the injunction, thus allowing a timetable to be formulated. Bids were called for, contracts eventually awarded, and construction resumed in late July of 1978, with a projected completion time for the bridge of sometime in 1981.

The original 1972 design of the bridge had been for a sort of trestle bridge, which many, including Gordon, found unacceptable. "At a recent lunch with Don Ketchum", Gordon says, "He said I was wrong in that. It never was to be that kind of bridge." As construction got under way, it became clear that it would be impossible to sink the bridge supports down to the bedrock level, which was something like 300 feet down and, therefore, too expensive to attempt. A modified design, then, called for a "friction" bridge, with pilings into the sand layer. This, according to Gordon, meant that "the muck" kept the bridge pilings from going down, but the pilings would not go up either.

5) Breaking ground for the bridge with Governor Carey

Gordon says, "Donald Ketchum, now retired, told me at that luncheon that, 'I remember the first contract I signed for the bridge, in round numbers, was $25,000,000. When it started up again, the contract I signed was for over $50,000,000.'"

"I had the privilege of breaking ground for the bridge[5] with Governor Hugh Carey," Gordon said. (This was in 1978.) While Carey was speaking and acknowledging those who had been instrumental in bringing the bridge "home," including Assemblyman Rolland Kidder, Chautauqua County Executive Joseph Gerace and Public Works Director William Parment—all Democrats, as was Carey—someone handed him a note and Carey said, "Also, I want to thank Legislature Chairman Gordon Anderson for his hard work getting this bridge built."

"I hadn't really done that much," Gordon says modestly.

Except that the bridge was in his district, he was the one who took the trouble to find out what constituents really wanted, and he constantly monitored what was going on. All of which was simply the way Gordon saw the job of representing a district of people and of working with a legislative team on issues of importance.

After the groundbreaking ceremony, the Governor said to Gordon: "I want to be bipartisan, so I named the mall in Albany after Nelson Rockefeller, and I want you to go to the county legislature and name this the Robert F. Kennedy bridge."

"I told him it would never pass and I wouldn't do it," said Gordon. And he didn't. When it was later brought to the legislature in a resolution and came to a vote, a proposal to name Interstate 86 the "Robert F. Kennedy Memorial Expressway" was defeated. The bridge is now called the Veterans' Memorial Bridge, an appropriate remembrance of the era when it was built, following the Vietnam War.

Car and occupants	50 cents
Truck up to 6 tons	35 cents
For anything above that	50 cents
4-wheel semi-truck	$1.00
Motorcycle	15 cents
Pedestrian	5 cents
Livestock, on foot, as riding horse	10 cents

6) Rates in 1950

During all the years while the bridge was waiting to be built, people still needed a way to get across the lake in preference to having to drive all around it. So the ferry was still a consideration.

Pedestrians	5 cents
Cars	40 cents
Motorcycles	25 cents
Pick-up trucks and trucks less than 1,200 pounds	55 cents
Trucks more than 1,200 pounds	80 cents
Trucks over 12 feet long	80 cents
Trucks with four-wheel trailers	$1.60
Livestock	10 cents

7) Rates in 1976

Throughout his legislative years, Gordon was involved in trying to keep the Bemus-Stow ferry in good service. The ferry itself was old and worn and needed repair or replacement. It had a record of losing money and no one could be expected to continue to operate it in the face of deficits. Yet, for all the while the bridge was enjoined, it was still the only game in town.

Several times in the 1970s the issue of ferry fares was addressed, and several times they were raised slightly. They were never exorbitant — hardly more even in the 1970s[6,7] than they had been in the early 19th century when the ferry began operation. The fare of 25 cents was eventually raised to 50 cents and there was an outcry.

At this writing, in part because Gordon Anderson represented one-half of the ferry district and kept tabs on what was going on and what was needed, the ferry is still running, in season, and it still provides an attractive, nostalgic and serendipitous way to get across the lake.

Meanwhile, the bridge was opened on October 30, 1982, with a span of 4,357 feet. People use it, now, without thinking, willingly, as a means of quick transport from Jamestown to the hookup with I-90 in Pennsylvania, and vice versa.

It is interesting to look back at some statistics connected with this bridge — now something of a Chautauqua County landmark. These are from a letter to Donald Ketchum, following a request from Gordon in 2003: "The 1973 contract to install piles for the bridge was for $24 million. After three piles were driven, the project was stopped due to environmental issues. The environmental review cost $1.2 million dollars. It cost $3 million to remove the three piles that were installed and another $12 million to 'buy out' the Phase I contract. Cost, at the time of construction, for the main bridge and ramps was $62 million. There was also $27 million for related highway work . . . The bridge type is steel multi-stringer. The foundation type is friction piles."

From the late State Senator Pat McGee's office, courtesy of Kevin Muldowney, come these figures on vehicle crossing traffic: In 1995, 8,550 drivers crossed the bridge; in 1997, 11,800, in 1998, 10,800, in 1999, 13,300; in 2001, 10,300; and in 2002, 11,000. And, again, according to Donald Ketchum, "there have been no actual truck traffic counts, but truck traffic is estimated at 8.5%."

Somehow, rather than being an eyesore or a means of polluting the beautiful ambiance that Chautauqua Lake still provides the area, the Chautauqua Lake Veterans' Memorial Bridge is simply one more way that the County of Chautauqua shows off its attractions. And, now, no one has to drive around half the lake to get from one side to the other.

PHOTO GALLERY-6

1) Bemus Point -Stow ferry with engine in the center

2) The ferry with the engine on the side to make room for another car

8) Looking East toward Shore Acres

9) Looking East from the halfway point

10) Looking East from Hadley's Bay

11) West from Bemus Point

12) Placing the steel girders

13) Laying the gridwork

14) Will East meet West?

PHOTO GALLERY-6

15) Installing the guard rails

16) Open to walkers on ribbon cutting day only

17) Aerial of finished project

18) View of Veteran's Memorial Bridge

19) Bird's Eye view of the bridge from Long Point

CHAPTER SEVEN

"WHAT TO DO ABOUT SOLID WASTE: THE FUTURE CALLS"

I n the early 1970s, when Gordon Anderson first took public office (as County Legislator representing District 5, comprising Ellery and Gerry townships), the issue of managing waste materials was heating up.

Anderson recalls, "My young sons loved the 'good old Ellery dump' as they called it. Often, when I would take a load of trash to the site, which was then on Walker Road, the boys would load stuff back on to the trailer as I unloaded our trash. They enjoyed rummaging for discarded toys and things others had thrown away. 'Boy, there's a lot of good stuff here Dad,' they would say. They were disappointed when the 'good old Ellery dump' closed in favor of the landfill."

Most citizens were now aware that pollution—of air, water, and the land—and what to do about solid wastes, and industrial and hazardous wastes, were serious problems. Lakes, including both Lake Erie and Lake Chautauqua, were "dying" because of being choked by polluting growth, in turn brought about by draining of phosphates and other pollutants into the waters.

Moreover, disposal of increasing amounts of discarded materials created crisis problems for the collecting sites around the county, most of which, in 1970, were open "dumps." It was becoming more and more obvious that better solutions had to be found.

There was a small flurry of interest in the early 1970s in inaugurating recycling operations to deal with materials, like plastics, glass, aluminum cans, and newspapers, which could be turned into reusable products. Such operations were small, however, and usually staffed by and dependent on volunteer cooperation. They were ineffective, in any case, unless there were nearby commercial operations, which could receive the materials and send them on for renewed processing. At least for the present, then, most waste materials would have to be disposed of in some other way than through recycling.

On December 8, 1971, the County Planning Board released the Havens and Emerson report titled Solid Wastes in Chautauqua County, A Comprehensive Planning Study, and subsequently took it out to a series of public meetings so as to educate the public.

In April of 1972, in Planning Director John Luensman's words, " . . .after much study and review of the public meetings, the Board recommended the report to the County Legislature for implementation."

In his Annual Planning Department Report for1972, Luensman quoted the following Planning Board's letter of recommendation:

"Based on the present state of the art, Chautauqua County must make a decision. Do the people of Chautauqua County desire to meet the minimum standards of Part 19 of the Health Code of the State of New York? If they have no desire to meet these standards, then there is no solid waste disposal problem. If there is a desire to meet the standards of the Health Code of the State of New York, then Chautauqua County has a problem.

"It is the belief of the members of the Planning Board that the concept that has been presented in this report is the least costly in terms of dollars and in terms of impact upon the environment. We believe that the recommendations of the report represent the least capital investment to be made to meet today's problem and that will allow us to transfer into any new technology at the least cost when one is found."

What the Board's letter (and Luensman) are referring to here is a landfill such as the one that would be proposed for the site in the Town of Ellery, where, incidentally, it now is, with state-of-the-art technology, ample space for growth, and adequate safety and security protection. Though a Town of Ellery site or others are not specified here in Luensman's report at the end of 1972, it did not take long, early in 1972, following those public meetings, for Chautauquans all around the county to begin protesting the idea of a solid waste disposal facility "in MY backyard."

Gordon Anderson again had the luck—if it can be called that—as he had had with the Driftwood campaign and the Chautauqua Lake bridge controversy of being smack in the middle of the area where the most frequently proposed solution would be located. Taking note of the rising tide of opposition in his district to a regional landfill in Ellery, he added a question on the landfill to his first survey of constituents, sent out in March of 1972, not long after he took office.

At a public meeting at Maple Grove High School on March 29, 1972, Gordon called the initial landfill site on Townline and Salisbury Roads in Ellery "inappropriate."

"It is especially amazing to me," he said, "that $127,000 plus or minus was spent on this study by the state and no soil samples have been taken in the proposed site areas. There may be good reasons for this, but it suggests sloppy research. And when I asked a question about the incline of the roads to the Ellery site at a public meeting at Southwestern High School, the engineer didn't even seem to be familiar with the area! It sounds as if this site was largely developed on paper."

Reporting on the survey of his constituents, Gordon said that on a question concerning the proposed landfill in Ellery, 54.5% of the respondents from Gerry and 82.5% of those in Ellery were against it.

"There were various reasons stated [for their opposition]," he said, "but one recurring one was: 'Landfill is not a good solution.'"

In concluding his comments, Gordon made three proposals:

"1. That the Public Works Committee of the Chautauqua County Legislature together with the County Department of Health make an onsite inspection of all county/town dumps and immediately initiate an interim plan which will close down the worst violators. This will help buy time.

"2. That Legislature Chairman Joseph Gerace appoint a special bipartisan legislative committee to tour other out-of-county installations to observe other types of operations such as using garbage to generate heat for electricity (which Jamestown could do), or incineration methods, or recycling, and to make a recommendation to the legislature concerning solid waste treatment.

"3. That my fellow legislators concur with me that in light of the poor access roads, the drainage problems, and the strong opinions of our citizens, we abandon all plans for a landfill operation in the Townline-Salisbury road area [the proposed Ellery site]." (The matter was resolved by locating the site on Towerville Road, where it operates efficiently today.)

Then, in both a press conference held on April 4, 1972, and in a letter to the Ellery Town Board dated April 11, 1972, Legislature Chairman Joseph Gerace discussed solid waste disposal problems. He said the present situation—the urgency of finding a solution to county waste disposal—came about because of NYS Health Department requirements. He said he felt that not one of the disposal sites now being operated in the county complied with state law. Further, he explained that some current sites were exhausted, so that communities would be forced to establish new disposal areas that complied with state requirements, or to bring present locations into compliance.

"Mr. Gerace said," the news story concluded, "that although the engineers' study [the Havens and Emerson Interim Plan] recommends primary and secondary landfill sites, test borings would have to be made to determine suitability for such use, such borings cannot be made without the property owners' consent, and the county could not justify condemnation of property unless it has been established it is suitable for the proposed use."

So here was a Catch-22 for the County: the urgency to get in compliance with the New York state health code; the dilemma of whether to rush construction of a new site or try to bring old, inadequate sites up to code; and, finally, the conflict between the need for test borings to determine a new site and the unwillingness of property owners to consent to those borings on their land. Added to this was the opposition in the Town of Ellery itself.

"There was no failure to inform the Ellery Town Board of intent to locate in the Town of Ellery," Gerace said in his letter to the Town Board, in an effort to pacify them.

"The Town Board of the Town of Ellery had a representative on the Solid Waste Disposal Committee which knew of the site long before the County Legislature did. Apparently there was a lack of communication. It is my understanding this Committee knew of the sites as long ago as January of 1971, and definitely knew as of October 1971."

It appears that Legislature Chairman Gerace felt the suggestions for interim action proposed by Gordon Anderson in March had merit for resolving some of the issues discussed above, and subcommittees for further study on waste disposal methods soon were functioning. Gordon's assignment was to chair the incineration study committee and to investigate incineration as a solution. Along with others he and Supervisor, Arden Johnson, visited Scio, NY, near Wellsville, where incineration was being used successfully, and he concluded and reported to the legislature repeatedly that incineration, with the use of "scrubbers", was the way to go in Chautauqua County because it was cleaner and less likely to present pollution problems in the future, and probably cheaper than landfill—and this in spite of the recommendations of the Havens and Emerson report.

All of this was taking time, as indicated by the annual reports. The County's own Solid Waste Committee Report had been submitted to the legislature in late 1971, and that year's report from the County Department of Health set as a goal for the future "that our environment be as pure as possible and free from air, water and solid waste pollution."

Yet, in the end-of-year report from the same agency in 1972, the Commissioner, Dr. Lionel L. Richardson, wrote:

"1972 was the [sic!] year of frustration in [the] attempt at developing a County-wide solution to solid waste management.

"An engineering study completed by Havens and Emerson Consulting Engineers in late 1971 was shelved by the County Legislature in favor of the development of a report by an 81-member Citizen's Committee formed by the Legislature in the spring of 1972.

"This report was completed and submitted to the County Legislature in late 1972 and it is hoped that action will be forthcoming in 1973 relative to implementation of a solid waste management plan in Chautauqua County."

Dr. Richardson then concluded, after department personnel had spent 192.75 "man-days" in surveillance of existing refuse disposal areas and trying to develop new sites, that "[t]he majority of refuse disposal areas in the County continue to be unsatisfactory, although some have shown improvement."

In 1973, accordingly, the Legislature got busy. At the regular meeting on February 9, members unanimously accepted Resolution No. 68-73, Adoption of a Comprehensive Solid Waste Management Plan, comprising those parts of the two studies "most applicable to meet the need of Chautauqua County." At the same meeting, through adoption of Resolution No. 71-73, they gave authorization to the Legislature Chairman to contract with and retain the services of appropriate engineering and management counsel for solid waste management as it went forward.

At their regular meeting on May 23, 1973, Emergency Resolution No. 225-73, adopted unanimously, authorized negotiation towards implementing "an interim plan" through the Public Works Committee by finding suitable sites for "initiating" the plan. (Note that none of this action specifically mentioned an Ellery site.)

By the June meeting, the legislature was authorizing the chairman to execute as necessary towards assuming responsibility for the operation and maintenance of all publicly owned landfill and dump sites in the County, "subject to the approval of the Legislature upon recommendation of the Public Works Committee."

In the meanwhile, a 1972 state law had provided financial aid for the construction of municipal solid waste management projects. Therefore, in August of 1973, a unanimously adopted resolution named the County of Chautauqua as such a "municipality" and authorized an application for a state grant-in-aid towards pursuing the solid waste management project, with the County assuming responsibility for remaining costs beyond what the state aid would cover.

At a subsequent special meeting, on August 30, the legislature adopted an official Policy Statement on Interim Solid Waste Plan (Resolution No. 356-73), though the decision had six dissenters. The policy would continue to guide the Solid Waste Committee, which had been operating informally for some time, and which was now formally ratified at the October 12 legislative meeting, and which would continue "until Phase I [of the Interim Plan] is fully implemented and operating."

A major change took place in 1973, as waste disposal became a county function, with the first County sites becoming operative in September. At the close of 1974, according to the County Health Report, there were six County refuse disposal sites, four individual municipal sites and four private demolition disposal sites, for a total of sixteen sites.

During the calendar year of 1974, efforts went forward towards implementing the Interim Plan for solid waste management, notably through the office and auspices of the Department of Public Works. The Legislature went along, taking care mainly of "housekeeping" details. They authorized negotiating contracts for soil test borings at prospective sites (March 8, 1974) and execution of license agreements in connection with these test borings (April 3); and acquired two sites, one in the Town of Chautauqua and one in the Town of Arkwright.

In another major development, the Legislature on October 29, 1974, passed a resolution authorizing Chairman Gerace and the Public Works Committee to apply to the New York Commissioner of Environmental Conservation for state aid for the planning of a comprehensive resource recovery (recycling) solid waste study for Chautauqua County. Then, in April 1975, Resolution No. 112-75, noting that the engineering firm of Gilbert Associates had been hired to conduct a study of ways to convert all of the County's solid waste to burnable fuel for the generation of power for the City of Jamestown, called for inviting interested private corporations to propose their solutions to this problem, and was referred to the Environmental Affairs Committee.

The annual report from the Division of Environment of the Department of Public Works noted that the County was continuing to meet the refuse disposal responsibility with existing sites, while continuing to identify possible sites for a permanent landfill. The study report from Gilbert Associates, originally planned for fall 1975, was delayed and was not expected until the spring of 1976.

The "Catch-22" dilemma referred to by Legislature Chairman Gerace in the spring of 1972 was now being resolved as the Legislature, on March 8, 1974, adopted Resolution No. 152-74, authorizing the Public Works Committee and the Legislature Chairman to negotiate and execute contracts at the various prospective solid waste landfill sites for soil test borings. This was augmented by Resolution No. 201-74, unanimously adopted on April 3, which authorized the chairs of the Public Works Committee and the Legislature to negotiate and execute licenses from property owners for the planned test borings.

So, the search for a permanent landfill site was going forward, and, simultaneously, the County, through a committee authorized by the legislature and the public works committee, applied once again to the State Commissioner of Environmental Conservation for funds to conduct "a comprehensive resource recovery solid waste study." The aim was eventually to recycle for future practical use as much of the County's refuse as possible, with a permanent landfill at a state-of-the-art level and with room for expansion ready to take whatever of that refuse could not be used in "resource recovery."

In April of 1976, the Legislature went on record with a resolution requesting New York State legislation, which would strengthen the power of Counties in the management and control of solid waste.

In May the Environmental Affairs Committee submitted a resolution — No. 147-76 — establishing rules and regulations for use of county landfill sites, including spelling out what could and could not be done in use of the sites, how the regulations would be enforced, what would be the penalties for violation, and the effective date: August 1, 1976. Surprisingly, the vote on the resolution was close: 13 yes and 10 no (Gordon Anderson voted with the affirmative). The resolution was referred to the Environmental Affairs Committee.

By October, the Legislature was refining solid waste management still further by passing unanimously a resolution calling for close coordination between the county and the city, town and village governments who use the landfills, and with private haulers, especially with regard to necessary closing of any sites. Then, in November, with another unanimous approval, the Legislature agreed to apply for a state grant-in-aid to be used for the planned solid waste management project.

In the annual report for 1976, from the Department of Public Works, Director William Parment submitted the lengthiest discussion to date of county landfill sites and uses thereof, including recycling. For the first time in these reports, the proposed Town of Ellery site was discussed, as follows:

"Options have been obtained for sufficient land to establish a sanitary landfill site in the Town of Ellery. Exploration has progressed to the point where we believe a site can be located here meeting satisfactorily the criteria [of the Department of Environmental Conservation]." This was in reference to the Towerville site.

Gordon Anderson had been active on many issues since he took office in 1972, and the solid waste management problem was one of them. On February 13, 1974, a public meeting was called by Town of Ellery officials to oppose the rumored Ellery site on Townline Road, the original proposed site which was different from the present Towerville site. Gordon had spoken at length in opposition, maintaining that constructing a new site in Ellery Township was in violation of the intent of the Havens and Emerson Interim Plan, of the intent of the Solid Wastes Study Committee, and of the intent of the County Legislature when it passed Emergency Resolution No. 225-73 in May of 1973.

Many of his constituents, as his surveys showed, also opposed development of an Ellery site for a landfill. In one of these surveys, he asked the respondents to list what they considered to be Chautauqua County priorities in the order of their preference. In both Ellery and Gerry, the top three priorities listed (out of a dozen or so issues) were, first, Chautauqua Lake pollution, which had county citizens very worried; second, the need for industrial development; and third, what to do about solid waste management. Yet at the same time, although the majority of the respondents supported landfill over incineration as a solid waste solution, they did not want the landfill at the Towerville Site—in their own backyard, as it were.

Things heated up again in 1977. On February 11, by a 15 to 8 vote, with two legislators absent and not voting, the legislature passed Resolution No. 52-77, authorizing purchase of 637.7 acres of land in the Town of Ellery for a proposed landfill site. Gordon was one of those voting no.

On September 9, the legislature approved by a 22 yes to 3 no vote Resolution #351-77, a bond resolution to facilitate financing of and carrying forward the Ellery landfill project. Again Gordon voted no. On December 16, a resolution authorizing purchase of land where a new access road to the site would be built was defeated by a 12 yes to 8 no vote, with five legislators absent (and therefore no clear majority of the legislature in favor). The tenor of this vote seemed to involve the fact that several legislators thought it was premature while still waiting for state permits and still experiencing citizen opposition to the Towerville site in the Town of Ellery. However, the exact resolution, with a new number, was passed on December 28 by 14 yes votes, 7 no votes (Gordon among them), and with 4 absent.

Then, as the legislature's final act in 1977, after a new body had been elected with, for the first time under the legislature umbrella, a Republican majority juxtaposed with a Democratic County Executive, they reconsidered the bond authorization resolution that had passed in September. The idea was to amend it to widen its coverage beyond the Towerville Landfill site to include other needy county projects. But the legislators, still worrying about pending state permits and citizen opposition, defeated the resolution as amended, by a 16 yes to 4 no vote, with 5 absent. A bond resolution required a two-thirds vote for passage, and the resolution's failure was bad news for those who worried about the long period of bringing the bond issue to fruition. Therefore, Ted Smith, in his own last act as legislator, asked that one of the dissenters consider changing his vote and asked that the resolution (No. 541-77) be reconsidered. Legislator Charles Barone complied and on the second vote the matter passed 18 to 2. Gordon Anderson and Perry Colburn were the two dissenters.

The landfill issue was especially troubling for Gordon because of his position in the center of the conflict, representing the majority of those opposed to the Towerville site. He was troubled by the fact that county departments were going ahead with purchasing property and other actions before the permits were in hand and the matter settled, and because he still felt that incineration and recycling might be a better way to go than landfill.

In fact, late in 1977, he wrote to Jack Glenzer, who was chair of the legislature's Environmental Affairs Committee, asking for a "complete review of the entire Ellery landfill matter." He asked that the committee consider the following questions: (1) Is one massive landfill the most efficient and economical method? (2) Is the site at Towerville necessary? (3) Regardless of what method or site is chosen, should the county run the operation? and, (4) What shall be the policy of the legislature concerning industrial waste?

Obviously, Gordon was hereby carrying forward his faithful representation of his constituents and his own conscience, but obviously, too, since he was already expected to be elected legislature chairman for the next term, he was also hereby seriously and responsibly taking on that mantle.

Gordon relates, "After I was elected Chairman in 1978, the EPA called me and asked if our landfill was completed. I said, 'No.' They said, in a rather nasty way, that they would take away funding. I retorted that, 'We are working on it and if you want to curtail funding, go ahead. By the time you get papers filed, we'll be finished.' I learned quickly that you had to be tough at times and that I could do it. They weren't going to push me around."

For all of 1978, the Ellery Landfill went forward towards completion and being opened as the official depository for Chautauqua County's solid waste, all that was leftover from recycling efforts. There is no mention of solid waste disposition, policy, or anything else in the official Proceedings of the Legislature for 1978 (though there is discussion and action on hazardous waste disposal) until page 545, in the annual report from the Division of Sanitation, signed by William Parment, Director of the Department of Public Works, where the following paragraph appears:

"Work was begun June 22, 1978 and continued for several months at the proposed Ellery Landfill site. Several acres were cleared of brush and stumps, a pole barn was built for equipment storage, and surveying was done and brush cleared for a new road off Towerville Road to the landfill site. The Highway Division has been building a compaction berm for the start of the landfill operations."

Strangely, it seems, after years of protest against a waste disposal site in Ellery Township, the whole thing had become a fait accompli. You might say that it was a battle that Gordon lost. In spite of everything, the landfill became a reality—in Ellery.

Since it's opening, the landfill has had two license renewals, now authorized until 2010. According to William Parment, there is room for expansion still for up to 80 years. Moreover, it is, in his opinion and those of others, an excellent facility—indeed a state-of-the-art example. What does Gordon Anderson think about it now that it has survived nearly 25 years?

"Over the years, the landfill became much more expensive than I ever envisioned. Million dollar cells must be used in part because the Jamestown water supply is near the bottom of the hill where the landfill is developed. In effect, the cells turn out to be time capsules with some decay going on inside but you are still left with a lot of bulk.

"The landfill does do some recycling, which is good. If incineration could have been used in addition to the landfill and recycling methods, I think we would have the best arrangement of all since some debris could be forever consumed.

"However, as humans, we live in an imperfect world and no system to control waste materials will please everyone."

PHOTO GALLERY-7

LANDFILL

1) The start of stripping away the soil

2) Building up the west side of the dike

3) The first "official" load of garbage

4) Second type of replacement gravel

96

CHAPTER EIGHT

MY ULTIMATE NEMESIS: SEWERING THE LAKE

Nothing in the political career of Gordon Anderson was more diffi-cult, more demanding, more frustrating or more elusive than the task of sewering Lake Chautauqua. Again, as with the landfill and the Chautauqua Lake Bridge, he was right in the middle of it all. He lived in and represented an area that would be part of the sewering if, and when, it was done. His term in the legislature—from 1972 through 1979—coincided with the years of crisis in the Center and South Lake sewer dis-tricts. And to cap it off, when he became chairman of the County Legislature, he was the CEO, so to speak, of both districts—until, for various practical reasons, he turned it over to the County Executive, Joseph Gerace.

At that point, state law required that chairpersons of County legislatures would be defacto chief executives of county sewer districts. Thus Gordon, once chosen as legislature chair, was in the hot seat but didn't entirely realize it. The Sewer Agency, with R. Theodore Smith as Chairman and John Luensman as Secretary, had been doing the week-to-week work. Anderson says that, even though he was Vice Chairman of the Sewer Agency, he never knew the project would be overdrawn with the Environmental Facilities Corporation. In addition, at that time (and still) county legislators held only part-time positions, receiving a salary that would in no way have given them a viable living wage. Therefore, like Anderson, most all of them held other "real-life" fulltime jobs, as has been previously stated. It was, then, a some-what astounding situation that he, employed as a fulltime college professor, and holding a demanding part-time position as a county legislator, should also, now, be taking on the almost unlimited workload as chairman of the County Legislature. There will be more about that, and its traumatic conse-quences, later.

As has been discussed earlier, pollution of the lake and its environs had been a problem for lakeside residents and the people of Chautauqua County ever since the first settlements of the area, though the sparse population in the early years prevented it from becoming a matter of crisis-control. Certainly, though, by the 1930s, concern for lake quality and safe drinking water was in many minds.

In fact, Gordon Anderson, has vivid memories of a polluted lake. He talks about swimming there as a very young boy about 10 years old and being aware, at times, that raw sewage was floating by, and of going out on the lake in a boat with his grandmother when he was very small, perhaps about 4 years old, to drop bottles and jars to the lake bottom as their means of getting rid of such throwaways. Most people, at that time, were not sensitive to the environment and the pollution that would ultimately result from their actions. Even the coal-fired steamers on the lake added to the pollution of it.

"I never dreamed at that point," he said, "that taking care of sewage and ridding the lake of pollution would be one of my [life's] contributions." The lake had been classified as "Grade A" in the late 1940s.

Yet even he did not really become concerned about raw sewage and its safe disposal until, as an adult with a family, he returned in the 1960s to a home overlooking the lake with deeded lake rights, and became involved in preserving the quality of life for himself and his family as users of the lake, and beyond, for his neighbors and fellow county residents.

Almost simultaneously with Gordon's return to Chautauqua County, efforts to deal with Chautauqua Lake's pollution began in earnest. In May of 1964 the *Jamestown Post-Journal* set out to inform the public of the extent of the problem. What focused attention on the situation was concern on the part of the County's Board of Supervisors about enforcing laws against lake pollution, evidenced by their consideration of a resolution to seek the state attorney general's opinion on who was or would be responsible for seeking such enforcement and for bringing charges against violators. Simple procedures were complicated by the fact that, although Chautauqua Lake is in Chautauqua County, the lake is actually owned by the state and used by others outside the county. It is also used as a facility and is depended upon for economic support by county residents. Moreover, jurisdiction might be the responsibility of any number of agencies or officers, including health officers, attorneys, the courts, or conservation agencies.

In an editorial dated May 12, 1964, the Post-Journal chided the Board of Supervisors for neglecting their responsibility for the lake's health and preservation.

What is needed today," the editorial said, "is an aggressive demand for action, the preparation of legislation which will give the County authority to establish a definite program with a county health and sanitary officer to enforce the movement and with the assurance of the backing of all county officials, including the Board of Supervisors."

The editorial further cited three responsibilities that the supervisors were "neglecting": that for the health of the residents of the county, that to "protect the natural assets of the County for [citizens'] enjoyment," and that "to economic progress of the County," as reflected in tourist trade and summer resort business.

Then, believing that "an enroused [sic] public should also be a well-informed public," the *Post-Journal* published a series of articles from May 13 through May 21 (1964), written by then City Editor Charles H. Pokrandt, in order to tell the complete story of the sorry state of the polluted lake. The article series was bolstered along the way by further editorials and by some graphic photographs of how sewage was being dumped into the lake.

By the end of the series, the newspaper was also able to carry a front-page story under the headline "Lake Association Acts: Attack Launched on Pollution," reporting that the private-citizen organization called the Chautauqua Lake Association (CLA) was taking the lead (not for the first time) in trying to solve the pollution problem. Since its founding in 1955, CLA had had its sights set on an unpolluted lake and its actions had ultimately led to formation of the Chautauqua County Sewer Agency in 1961. Yet four years later the agency was still little more than a name and there were no sewers in sight.

A month after running the article series in 1964, the Post-Journal, in another editorial, noted that virtually nothing had been forthcoming from the state in help with the pollution problem and that it appeared responsibility would now fall to the towns and the county. Especially those towns bordering the lake would be asked to prepare their own anti-pollution ordinances and the mechanism for enforcing them. In addition, the *Post-Journal* called again for a county health district with "a strong and able health officer to lead the movement."

The County Health Department came into being, after a state Public Health Law mandate, through County Legislature Resolution #124-64, "Establishing a County Health District," on August 14, 1964. A governing Board of Health was then authorized by resolution on October 16, 1964. At this point environmental health was not specifically mentioned as part of either philosophy or goal of the new Health Department. However, a separate section called "Environmental Health," in the department's report for 1965, cited problems for the county with sewage disposal, safe water, compliance with the New York State Sanitary Code, sewage treatment plants, safe swimming, and other matters. The section also noted "but a new site for a sanitary landfill has not been found."

The Environmental Health Services report for 1966 said that a master plan for the development of sewerage facilities for the entire county was being developed, with the plan expected by June 1, 1968; and that there were also in the works master plans for water supply development and for disposal of refuge, noting especially the present "haphazard development for refuge disposal around Lake Chautauqua."

Further, the report said: "This is a time when we cannot afford to make mistakes, nor can we afford not to act, for we are laying the basic foundation for the future environmental health of this county."

Map of the sewer districts surrounding Chautauqua Lake, 2003

This map shows the public and private sewer districts serving customers around Chautauqua Lake. Note the amount of shoreline, particularly on the western side, that is not served by public sewers. The North, Center and South Sewer Districts were formed and built in the 1970s and 80s and are operated by Chautauqua County. Chautauqua Institution has had its own sewer district for many years. The "private" sewer districts along the northeastern lakeshore serve two large condominium developments. The "gap" along the shoreline on the southeastern side of the lake is the John Cheney farm.

(Source: South and Center Chautauqua Lake Sewer Districts)

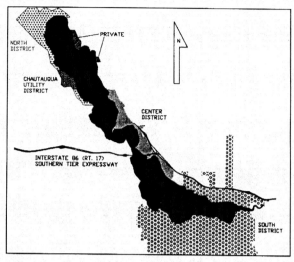

1) Sewer districts, indicated by gray areas

Little did anyone know at that point of the "mistakes" and "inaction" that lay ahead in connection with sewer development in Chautauqua County.

"Sewering the lake" began to move again in 1967 when, according to a chronology published once again in the Post-Journal, Chautauqua County signed a contract with Metcalf and Eddy of New York, Inc. (an engineering firm) to do a state-financed "Comprehensive Sewerage Study for all of Chautauqua County." Both the county Board of Supervisors and the state Health Department accepted the resultant study in 1968, and the annual report for that year noted that, "intensive promotional activity will have to be undertaken on all levels of government to obtain popular support of projects to implement this study."

There were implications from this study for the entire county. In the next years, sewer projects would be carried out not only around the badly polluted and dangerously threatened lake, as represented by four separate districts[1], the North Lake District, the Center Lake District, the South Lake District[2], which would hook up with the facilities of the city of Jamestown and expand into its western lake suburbs, and a separate sewering of Chautauqua Institution and its immediate environs, but also through the north part of the county with a Pomfret-Portland-Dunkirk district and a separate accommodation for a newly developing Northern Industrial Park to the east of the City of Dunkirk.

For each of these individual projects all the steps—from study to contracts to construction and finish—had to be inspected and accepted by the various state agencies involved. These could, and did, include, the Environmental Protection Agency (EPA); the Department of Energy Conservation (DOC), at both the state and federal levels; the State Legislature; the Governor (by implication if not actually in fact) and even the

Park and Recreation Division of the New York State Historical Review Section. At any or all of these agency levels the process could, and often did, take months. And if, by some chance, a bureaucrat at any of these agencies allowed the documents to languish on a desk or shelf, forgotten, more months could pass. Sometimes an agency would ask for more information, or in some cases the question had, by state law, to be put to referendum, causing still more delays. In these early years, then, the preliminaries dragged on and because of new requirements, for environmental impact studies and/or archeological clearing, and inflation, the projected costs of the combined Center and South Lake sewers and the Celeron treatment plant rose from around $9.6 million in 1969 to $17.3 million in 1972, and there were still no sewers being built.

An entry for 1969 in the *Post-Journal* chronology says that, "the county Sewer Agency contracted with the state Pure Water Authority to help prepare reports on forming [two sewer districts—the Center district and the South district]. The Pure Water Authority, later called the Environmental Facilities Corporation, was eventually hired by the sewer agency to construct, own and operate the facilities of the two districts over the life of the bonds used to pay for the facilities. When the bonds are paid off at the end of 40 years, the facilities would revert to the districts." (Basically, it was a "turn-key" agreement.)

Both the county and the state approved the plans for the Center District; the South District was approved after a referendum held in November 1969.

In 1970, the county legislature hired two firms to do reports on the two sewer districts, Metcalf and Eddy (again), for the South District, and William Cosulich Associates, for the Center District. The reports for both districts were sent to the state in January of 1971. The Center district report was approved in June, but more information was requested for the South District, resulting in approval by the state in September.

In November 1971, after a four way primary, Gordon Anderson was elected to the new County Legislature, which was replacing the old Board of Supervisors. He would represent District 5, comprised of Ellery and Gerry Townships. (At this point the legislature could still include, if elected, members who were also town supervisors, though that double-office tenure was later phased out.) In that first legislature, as has been previously discussed, there were 25 members, and Gordon early on emerged as one of its leaders.

In an interview for the *Post-Journal* shortly after his election, Gordon was quoted as follows: "My own 'priorities schedule' places the Chautauqua Lake sewer very high. I love the lake. It is our major asset. While we badly need the expressway, I must admit I would not trade the sewer for the bridge and suggest an alternate route for the expressway over the top of the lake. I am also convinced that the county badly needs a full-time county executive. I believe he would more than pay for himself if he is skilled." [Note that at this point there is still the assumption that any such executive would be male.]

(It should be noted that the county executive position did come to be written into the county charter, and, in the election of 1974, Joseph Gerace was elected to be the first holder of that office.)

Progress towards sewers around the lake remained a priority for Gordon throughout his legislative career. With Gordon in the legislature and sewers his priority, there was a bonanza in the offing: in 1972, federal legislation authorized a $24-billion water-cleanup program which included collection water systems. This meant that to qualify for federal funds, the county would have to design plans for a collection system, something that had not yet been done.

Still to be fixed were the user costs, and there were differences around the districts because some areas already had collection systems while some didn't. Moreover, since there were more people to be covered in the South District, the costs for Center District residents would be higher than those of the South District.

In November of 1972, in another referendum, voters approved the state's $1.5-billion bond issue and Congress passed the $24-billion program, known as the Clean Water Bill, to help improve the environment.

For Gordon Anderson it might have seemed that sewers were definitely "on the way." But no. President Richard Nixon vetoed the Clean Water Bill and Congress overrode him. In retaliation, Nixon impounded the money, declaring the bill "inflationary," and he then released only $3 billion.

Meanwhile, the Clean Water Bill required that the Celeron treatment[3] plant, under construction, "offer partial tertiary treatment to waste water" which, alone, would raise the cost by about $1 million. To further complicate matters, the federal Environmental Protection Agency (EPA), created in 1969, began to demand environmental assessment and impact statements before money

4) Joseph Gerace, Anderson, John Lunensman, Art Carlson at the Ground breaking, Sept 26, 1976

could be given out to build such things as sewer systems. The Sewer Agency was stunned.

By 1974, after an EPA assessment was approved, the cost of Chautauqua County's sewer-the-lake effort was projected to cost a phenomenal $23 million. The sewers were still not being built, but in 1975 a New Jersey challenge resulted in lifting Nixon's embargo on the Clean Water funds, and New York was slated to receive $1 billion. The $23 million cost-projection for

Chautauqua Lake sewers remained stable, but while the state and federal government would pay for 87.5 percent of the project, none of the funds could be used for collection systems, which the local districts would themselves have to fund.

Then, very, very belatedly, the New York Archeological Council filed an injunction stopping work on 55 sewer projects in the state, including both the South and Center Chautauqua districts, until an archeological survey could be done. As luck would have it, some alleged artifacts were found within Chautauqua boundaries and there were further delays while the claims were investigated.

6) Gordon, Jim Mead, Tony Raffa as Gordon accepts the chairmanship

Although federal grants were awarded for beginning the treatment plant in Celeron and, in stages, for the South and Center district construction, still another archeological challenge interfered, and it was 1977 with still no sewers in sight.

By now Gordon Anderson, like others who had been working on the sewer projects for years, was stymied. Since at least 1976 Gordon[4,5] had been asking that a sewer project administrator be hired, to insure some professional and responsible oversight. In addition, it was now clear that the Environmental Facilities Corporation (EFC) had made several costly mistakes in its planning and production, and that drastic action was needed to save the project. Moreover, the money had run out and contractors could not be paid, and the sewer train was screeching to a halt.

From January 1978, Gordon, as chairman of the County Legislature[6] was, by law, the executive in charge of the sewer projects. At one point, while Gordon and his wife were on a long weekend vacation, he got a call from Charles Barone, County Legislature Clerk, who was calling at the urging of County Executive Gerace. A letter from the EFC, addressed to Anderson, had been received. Legislature Clerk Barone had been given permission to open mail that came during Gordon's absence.

"Would you authorize $7 million to be sent to EFC to cover the overdrafts?" Barone asked.

Gordon said, "No", and Barone said, "Nor would Gerace."

Gordon recalls, "I directed Barone to advise the Legislature that there would be an emergency meeting called, cut our little vacation short and quickly returned home. As soon as I could I convened the emergency meeting of the legislature. Gerace said, 'It looks like the project will be shut down.'

I had thought certain people were going to be carrying the ball, but it seemed like everyone was throwing their opinions against the sewer. That's when I felt like the boy in Hans Brinker with his finger in the dike—the only one holding back the flood of disaster."

Others, including Angelo Bennice and Charles Barone, agree with Gordon that the project would have collapsed if he hadn't exercised his leadership and "hung in there."

Finally, in 1978, Angelo (Ange) Bennice had been hired as Administrative Director of the South and Center Sewer District projects, still under the aegis of sewer district boards. Gordon describes a "very tough meeting" at the airport to try to resolve the contract and money problems.

"Ange and I were there, along with some others," he said, "and big labor and big business were there, too. I kept saying to them that the legislature had now passed the $6 or $7 million so everyone would get paid. We were not allowed to take any minutes and if we did they would refuse to negotiate. They promised me they would stay on the job, but after a while they walked off the job anyway."

Bennice takes up the story: "When I came on board, the two projects (South and Center) were targeted to be completed at a cost of $55 million. The Environmental Facilities Corporation was still manager of the whole project and they had hired Metcalf and Eddy from Boston and William Cosulich Associates to do the construction. They proceeded to go to construction and the first thing they encountered in the main treatment plant was that they ran into poor soil conditions. Where they were planning on using wooden pilings, they found that the wooden pilings were just sinking right out of sight because they had relied on some old data of some borings they had taken. [Anderson interjects, 'There were only three borings, as I remember and they hit only high points.']. So they had to execute a change order, which was approved by EFC in the amount of $5 million, to go to steel pilings. That was the first snafu in the project. Then they put out some other contracts for bid and they found these contracts were coming in 100 or 200 percent over the estimates.

"So when I came on board, my first recommendation was to fire EFC. I thought they were incompetent. I'd done an independent analysis estimate with a friend of mine out of Cleveland (He was a partner in a consulting firm). We got an estimate of what this project would cost and we came up with a cost estimate of something like 73 or 75 million dollars."

Because of conflicting opinions and bids coming in that seemed to be proving that the EFC cost estimate was nowhere near the mark, even after the years of planning and hope, collapse seemed imminent.

At this point, Bennice says, the county finally decided to bring a lawsuit against EFC and the engineers Metcalf and Eddy. They won the lawsuit and settled for 2.1 million dollars.

In 1979, Bill Parment and Anderson went to Port St. Lucie, Florida to observe the workings of a vacuum system. As a result, the county decided to hire the firm of O'Brien and Gere to carry the project forward. In the wake of the failure of the wooden pilings and the unlikelihood that gravity sewers could do the job, because they were all horizontal with pump houses lifting the sewage, (and the farther along, the deeper they must go), Bennice urged O'Brien and Gere to consider vacuum sewers which had been approved in the early Fall of 1979.

"Take a good look," Bennice said. "Let's go out to Rochester, Indiana, where the factory is and talk to those officials and see their demonstration project. Bring all your top people and make a decision for yourselves."

"We went out there," Bennice said, "and they were so impressed that they designed the rest of the project. It was very successful. At one time we had one of the largest vacuum sewer systems in the country. [Some] were saying the life expectancy of those sewers was seven years. Those valves were put in in 1985 and here it is 2004 (almost 20 years later) and they're still working beautifully."

Much of the sewer battle had been in the legislature. (It should be noted that, at roughly the same time, the northern part of the lake, involving Mayville, Dewittville, and parts of Chautauqua Township was successfully sewered with little trouble and conflict, operating under a completely separate sewer district board. The Northern project started after the South and Center project and was finished before the South and Center project was completed, which underlines the many problems of the South and Center District.)

The hiring of Angelo Bennice caused some of the flak against the legislature to dissipate. Still, there were required public hearings and, at some of them, citizens, angry mainly at the inflation in the costs of building the sewers and the concomitant rise in their projected user fees, exhibited the kind of hostility that can make such meetings nightmares for the elected and appointed officials responsible for whatever was being discussed.

However in 1977 the Sewer Agency gave chairman Ted Smith the power to sign contracts with EFC to carry the work forward, which he did, but a requirement that there must first be public hearings authorizing such action was overlooked. It was up to the legislature chairman, then Frank Bratt, to call such a hearing. The fact that it had not been done was not discovered until 1978, after Gordon had become legislature chairman. This oversight, in Gordon's words, "caused all kinds of problems, finally involving getting to the State Legislature, requiring them, in effect, to back-date our letting the contracts."

Gordon, who was constantly in the forefront at such moments, experienced more than his share of hostility while acting as a responsible representative, not only of his district but of the citizens throughout the county.

Through these years, he and his family were harassed by angry letters, threatening phone calls, and even death threats. In one case, he received a letter from a (presumed) constituent, threatening to kill not only Gordon and the Ellery Town Supervisor, Arden Johnson, but their wives as well.

As with other fees that might be assessed from county residents—any proposed fees for lake quality management, for instance—the sewer fees caused friction. For one thing, the fees would vary from property to property depending on location and distance from the sewer line. Secondly, not all properties in all the districts to be served would be attached to the sewers; and third, even those citizens who would not be served by the sewers, but would retain their own septic tanks would, in many cases, still have to pay a smaller sewer fee. It was difficult to convince all the people of the need for sewers around Chautauqua Lake, and the fee structure was still in the talking stage. (One letter that Gordon received, presumably from a constituent who did believe that sewers were needed, complained at length about the pollution of the lake, saying at one point that the lake "is nothing but a skeptic tank." Freudian slip or not, the letter made its point.)

Finally, in October 1978, after consultation with County Executive Gerace and his fellow legislators, Gordon Anderson introduced resolutions to turn executive administration of the South and Center sewer projects over to the County Executive. Anderson emphasizes that this arrangement was by his wish and was more practical because the County Executive had a staff to handle the load and Anderson did not. County Executive Gerace was in agreement.

"Although Joe, in comments to the press and speeches 'on the stump,' made it seem that he had taken it over because I couldn't handle it, I had in fact suggested it to him and had initiated a solution that was needed in the face of that emergency. We had equipment and partly finished construction at the Celeron plant that needed to be protected for the winter or we'd incur still more enormous costs, and we had to get the job going again.

"You have to realize that this was a huge amount of money—as Angelo Bennice testified, it was $78 million at that point—a huge responsibility for a part-timer with no staff. If I had continued to be in charge, we'd have had to hire more staff, while the County Executive was full-time and he had a staff to help with the work. It seemed like a good move, although many were angry with me."

At this same time, through another resolution, the county invoked "police powers" in order to get everything moving. This brought criticism from the press and others. The *Post-Journal* said taking police powers was "a dangerous step," but also recalled that Gordon Anderson had in 1976 been warning of a dire situation developing which would require drastic action to fix and that no one had listened. Still the resolution invoking these powers passed the legislature unanimously, and within a few months the action had been ratified when Governor Hugh Carey signed into law a bill authorizing such action in emergencies. Thus, the county got through the sewer crisis.

Bill Parment, who was very much involved, in one way or another, with the progress of county government from the late 1960s (see his comments in the Foreword at the beginning of this book), was one of the keenest of observers as the sewer troubles mounted through the early 1970s. He was Director of Public Works at the time that the legislature turned the authority for the sewer projects over to the County Executive.

At this point, Parment says, "Mr. Gerace asked me to take over the project and bring it in to completion." Parment describes in his own graphic terms the floundering: First the engineering firm, Metcalf and Eddy, errs by failing to take borings to measure the plasticity of the soil at the sewage treatment plant in Celeron. Next, the design is flawed because of the failure to take the proper borings. In a domino effect, then, the piling work fails and costs escalate. Contracts, which have already been let cannot be carried out, resulting in delays and additional escalating costs. The citizens of the county[7], required to authorize the projects through referenda, became, as Parment puts it, "so fed up with the project that they wouldn't vote for the increase in needed money." The county stopped paying the contractors, who in turn left the job site and the whole ten years or more of work was in danger of collapse.

Eventually, as history has proved, the completion did occur[8,9]. In 1985 sewers were operating around Chautauqua Lake and, as Angelo Bennice says, they are still working well, and they have a projected 100-year lifespan, which should pacify most critics.

As Gordon Anderson puts it, the Chautauqua Lake sewer projects became a dominant crisis in his life. At one point, he says, what with sleepless nights, citizen hostility, and days filled with attempts at peacemaking and peacekeeping, with difficult decisions and executive action, he did feel overwhelmed.

While many, many other Chautauqua county citizens contributed much to the eventual success of the sewer-the-lake projects, Angelo Bennice, Joseph Gerace, Bill Parment, the late John Luensman, R. Theodore Smith and Gregory Yaw among them, Gordon Anderson, the finger-in-the-dike man, whom many others credit as the responsible legislator who wouldn't give up, now has the satisfaction of knowing that the sewers are in place and the lake is still alive and well.

PHOTO GALLERY-8

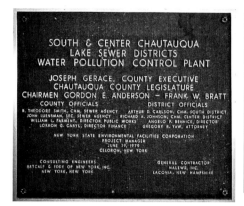

2) South & Center Sewer Control Plant

3) Celeron Sewage Plant

5) JCC Professors at groundbreaking L to R; Robert Barber, Gordon, Bill Cotter, Bob Sundhill, Royal Stubing, Ted Smith and son Kevin, Ed Cherry, Marion Panzarilla

• The Concerned Citizens of Chautauqua County had sent letters to all property owners in the South and Center Chautauqua Lake Sewer Districts to ensure that they know they are included in the sewer districts and advise them that there are several hearings and decisions coming up that would affect them. The letters predicted there would be a "blitz of misleading information" prior to hearings and noted that the Concerned Citizens wanted to "counteract" this information by keeping them informed of the "true status" of the project.

7) From the Post Journal, October 1979

8) Excavating for the Center District sewer lines at Lakecrest

9) Dick Johnson, a member of the sewer committee, surveys the digging on his property at Lakecrest

CHAPTER NINE

THE CHALLENGES OF LEADERSHIP

ot every leader is a Leo—i.e., born under the sign of the lion between July 24 and August 23—but many Leos do become leaders. Gordon Anderson, born on August 3, is one of them. Not to put undue emphasis on the influence of astrological happenstance, obviously something was at work in this man from the time of his youth. That Swedish political organizer who was his great-grandfather contributed, no doubt, as did the fact that, as Christie Herbst, Editor of the *Post Journal* put it, with affection, Gordon illustrated, in good ways, the stereotypical "stubborn Swede."

"Me being me," is the way Gordon describes it, as he recounts his experience in the front rank with the Driftwood Campaign, county reapportionment, the Chautauqua Lake Bridge, the "battle" over the Ellery landfill, the Swedish exchange program at JCC, and, of course, the long, long troubles over trying to get sewers around the lake.

Whatever the ultimate cause, or causes, there is no doubt that Gordon Anderson emerged as a force to be reckoned with in the governance and quality of life in Chautauqua County in those exciting days of the 1970s—and before and beyond.

He was elected to political office on his first time out , in 1971, as we know, taking his seat on behalf of County District 5 in the first ever County Legislature on January 1, 1972. That legislature had a Democratic majority of 15, and at the January 3 organizational meeting, Joseph Gerace, Supervisor of the Township of Busti, was elected as Legislature Chairman by a vote of 14 to 9, with two abstaining. For that legislative session, Frank Bratt, Democrat from District 6 (Jamestown), was appointed Majority Leader and Hamilton Clothier, Republican from District 3 (Silver Creek), was appointed Minority Leader.

From the beginning, Gordon Anderson was a presence to be counted on both in the discussion of issues and in the voting on resolutions. It is also noteworthy that, for his entire service during four terms covering eight years, Gordon was seldom absent from the meetings of the legislature and its committees, or from the necessary public hearings and side events where the legislators' presence was either desired or required. In 1979, the Post-Journal took notice of the fact that Gordon Anderson and Joseph Lepkowski were the only two legislators who had attended all their assigned legislative meetings during 1978. Through diligence and faithful presence, therefore, Gordon was throughout a leading legislator.

It wasn't long, however, before his leadership began to show itself in other significant ways. In initiating, signing on, and introducing resolutions on serious issues, for instance. In his first term (January 1972-December 1973), he teamed up with Legislator Theodore Smith (in May of 1972) to introduce and sponsor resolutions on requiring a study of alternate routes for the Southern Tier Expressway to avoid building a bridge over Chautauqua Lake and on informational action so the Chautauqua County voters could decide on whether to support an Environmental Quality Bond Act (1972) which would help to fund the Center and South Chautauqua Lake Sewer Districts. Both resolutions passed.

Subsequently, on September 27 and September 28, 1972, hearings for residents of both the Center and South Districts were held to inform people of the plans for going ahead with the sewers. At the Center District hearing, Gordon revealed the results of a survey he had taken in his district, with respondents from both Gerry and Ellery in favor of proceeding with the Center District Sewer. As noted by both news reports and editorial comment in the *Post-Journal* and Dunkirk's *Evening Observer*, this was the first time in county government that a legislator had undertaken to poll his district's voters about their opinions on governmental matters concerning themselves and their district.

Later that year (in November), a resolution on proceeding with completion of the Southern Tier Expressway was unanimously adopted, and both the late Ted Smith and Gordon spoke in favor of it on the grounds that sufficient information to the citizens of the county had been provided.

The first year of Gordon's first term had been an important one, with nearly all the issues addressed on which he would take a leadership role. The legislature authorized the first comprehensive Solid Waste Management Study; the Chautauqua Lake Benchmark Study, in contract with the State University College at Fredonia, with help from personnel at Jamestown Community College; and the resolutions towards progress on the Southern Tier Expressway and the Chautauqua Lake Bridge and on both the Center and South Sewer District projects mentioned above.

In the 1973 calendar year, with legislature organization and function running, now, smoothly, many important actions were taken. The group worked to strengthen the Industrial Development Agency—important for improving the economic health of the County; and the county's health department overview, especially of mental health. A county office of public works was authorized in March, with overseeing public sanitation (involving solid waste disposal) included. In May, the legislature passed Local Law #7-1973, establishing the Chautauqua County Office of the Aging—the first such county agency in New York State.

The legislature and the various government functionaries, such as the County Attorney, the Planning officer and planning board, the department of public works and the county health department, faced up to the fact that emerging Federal and State laws and environmental standards now required taking responsibility for solid waste management and acting against further pollution of Lake Chautauqua. Therefore, in Resolution 265-73, adopted June 27, 1973, authorizing the Chairman of the Legislature to sign leases to implement a solid waste plan, there was this wording: "That the Chairman of the Legislature be and hereby is authorized to execute such papers and documents as may be necessary for the County of Chautauqua to assume responsibility for the operation and maintenance of *all publicly owned landfill and dump sites in Chautauqua County*, subject to the approval of the Legislature upon recommendation of the Public Works Committee." (Italics by this author.)

In further action to implement steps towards fulfilling an official policy on solid waste disposal and beginning work on an interim waste disposal plan in August 1973, while the legislative members were discussing six resolutions on these matters, Gordon Anderson demonstrated a trait that he became much recognized for—his "bringing-people-together" role. Just before the votes were taken on the six resolutions, he said:

"I think now we've talked about it long enough and we ought to get on with the voting. We all know how we feel, and I hope we'll all exercise a little courage to try to do what's best for the County over all."

Although the resolutions were not unanimously approved, all six did pass with sizeable majority votes, and there were people from both parties on both sides of the votes.

In the meantime Gordon was re-elected to the legislature for two more terms, in 1973 and 1975, with sizeable vote margins in both cases. He had, two more times, surveyed his constituents to get their opinions on location of a landfill, whether to build a bridge over the lake, problems of the ferry, and other issues. And he had initiated a column that ran in the *Westfield Republican* to give his constituents and other county residents the "straight goods" on issues that people were vocal about. Moreover, through his entire legislative service he was open to hear the views and concerns of those he represented.

As he worked to be a good political representative, he was sensitive to the needs of the constituency which the legislature, and all of county government, served. Early on he successfully led a movement to have all legislative meetings open to the public—not just the general meetings but all committee sessions as well. Cognizant, too, of how often hypocrisy colored the actions of political representatives, Gordon twice refused a raise in pay that would have been coming to him through legislative authorization. In both cases—in October of 1972 and when he took over as chairman in 1978—he felt that because he had voted against both raises he should not benefit from the result.

Perhaps, though, the next most publicized and controversial leadership stance he took was in proposing a lake management district to alleviate the problems of lake pollution and clogging of passages by overabundant plant growth in the lake. By his own testimony, Gordon had known about lake pollution and its causes from his earliest days, and he had always followed closely what was going on in efforts to deal with maintaining the quality of the lake. He was much influenced by such things as a report, part of the "Benchmark Study" of the lake, called "Chautauqua Lake: A Report to the Public, Vol. I: The State of the Lake," issued shortly before he proposed his Lake Management District. The study began by comparing "benchmark data": results from a survey done of the lake in 1937, compared with results obtained by studying the lake from 1971 through 1975. The study reported:

"The lake's weed communities today are quite different from what they were in 1937. Weeds were prevalent then, but a more favorable ecological balance existed among them. Competition between at least a dozen different species of weeds prevented pest varieties from becoming dominant. [Now] this weed diversity has been lost . Two species now dominate the lake each summer and have become a problem to users of the lake. These two are curly leaf pondweed and water milfoil. Similar studies have been carried out on lake algae. In 1937, diatom algae were dominant in Chautauqua Lake throughout the year. This desirable condition no longer exists . . . .Instead, green and blue-green algae predominate from late spring though late fall— the latter species causing undesired lake scum, "pea soup" conditions, and offensive odors. A third area of study has involved aquatic animal life . We have found that the taxonomic diversity or richness among these organisms today is about half of that present in 1937."

The report also discussed the state of the lake's water transparency, which it said also had declined measurably since 1937. And the study had "developed a comprehensive body of data describing in detail the chemistry of lake water and of the tributary streams that feed the lake. This information," it said, "will prove to be useful 'benchmark' data to monitor future changes in the lake and streams."

And it concluded: "By and large this work shows that water quality in Chautauqua Lake is good, that its chemistry is well within established drinking water standards, and that the lake is safe and well-suited for recreational use and sports fishing. Our research work, however, suggests that there is a marked trend toward increasing rates of production of undesirable algae[1] and weeds. This trend constitutes the principal problem of the lake."

Such expert information, along with the knowledge that, increasingly, raw sewage flowing into the lake was a significant cause of pollution of the

1) Algae may not necessarily be pollution, but often is

County's major asset, led Gordon to want to use his influence to do something about the lake's problems. He felt permanent lake maintenance and sewers were the answer.

Although a master's thesis from 1977 claims that someone else first proposed such a lake district, according to Gordon's own memory and corroboration in newspaper accounts and editorials from February 27, 1976 through March of the next year, clearly Gordon did initiate the proposal for a permanent lake management district. He called several meetings of lakeside residents, county officials, state legislators and other county citizens to discuss such a district and chaired a committee which worked with County Planning Director John Luensman and County Attorney Edwin Kuzdale to come up with a plan for implementing lake management. Throughout, Gordon tried to assess the wind changes of public opinion about the matter, and tried to address the central questions. He noted that the problem of lake maintenance existed because, although the state of New York owns the lake, it does not control or maintain it. The sticking point, too, he knew, was how to raise the funds needed for permanent maintenance. The only real possibility was some sort of levied tax, but any mention of that led to hot opinions over whether only those who lived on the lake, or the entire citizen body of the county, or, even beyond that, the visitors from elsewhere in the state and outside the state who used the lake should all be assessed.

In his newspaper column, "In My Opinion," he discussed the problem, noting that people who lived on the lake were worried that they alone would be forced to bear the burden for maintaining the lake. "But don't worry," he assured his constituents. "Your representatives won't sell you out."

However, in March of 1977, the *Post-Journal* reported that the Lake Management District was now "dead," as the result of the County Legislature's Environmental Affairs Committee voting down a proposal to pursue New York State approval for the District plan. As could have been predicted, a main reason for the plan's failure was an impasse on how to fund it. Also by that time even Gordon was not sorry to see the plan's demise, because he now knew that there were plans in the works to dredge some heavily silted sections of the lake, to repair the Warner Dam controlling the outlet of the lake and to dredge the Chadakoin outlet itself—all actions that would help considerably in alleviating the lake's problems. Moreover, the Central and South Sewer district projects were now, supposedly, back on track and these also would eventually ease lake pollution. It is likely, however, that Gordon's leadership of the anti-pollution effort during his 1976-1977 term had considerable influence towards moving all these projects forward. The effect on quality of life in the County is ultimately immeasurable when all such efforts are taken into account.

Perhaps the activity through 1976 in connection with the lake district proposal was one of the reasons that Gordon was proposed for, and appointed as, minority leader of the legislature at the organizational meeting in January of 1977. Up to that time, in Gordon's service in the legislature, the Democrats had been in the majority and the chairman of the legislature, consequently by dint of the majority vote, had been a Democrat (Joseph Gerace from 1972-74 and Frank Bratt from 1975, when Gerace became County Executive, through 1977).

When Gordon became minority leader, he was able to refine his ideas on what it meant to serve in a legislature that, although composed of members from two parties, inevitably had one party in the majority and one in the minority. "When you're in the minority," he said, "you don't have to work so hard. It's a lot different when you get to be in the majority—then you really have to deliver."

As he put it in the statement quoted by Christie Herbst in the introduction to this chapter (from George Orwell's novel *Animal Farm*), "All animals are equal, but some animals are more equal than others." Yet he knew that among the "unequal animals" in the Democratic-dominated legislature he was growing in "equality."

When Frank Bratt gave his speech in response to being elected majority leader on January 1, 1975, he began by saying: "Fellow legislators, Ladies and Gentlemen: I couldn't agree with Gordon Anderson more that we need the two party system and need to keep it alive. We had 150 years of a one party system in this county and in the last three years we've had a two party system. We have come alive in this county, and in '75 we hope to keep alive."

Such a reference to a fellow legislator of the opposing "stripe" was singular. But, as Gordon recalls: "I think I was starting to be quite effective and in 1977, there was no question that I was the "most powerful legislator," as someone dubbed me in the newspaper. I was very active. I was involved in the road-building and the subsequent debate over pollution in the lake and the press was solidly behind me."

Moreover he had served on the County sewer board, as vice chairman throughout, since before being elected to the legislature. He was on the Solid Waste Committee, serving as chairman of the Incineration subcommittee. He had led the effort to find a solution to the problem of keeping the ferry running across the lake. When you turned this way or that in looking at what county government was doing, Gordon was always involved somehow.

When asked why he had chosen to run as a Republican, he replied, "Well, you have to run as something and my philosophy is Republican, my parents and grandparents were Republican and the person that I replaced as legislator candidate was Republican, so . . . But as a practical matter, if you look at my voting, I tended to be a fiscal conservative, but I was more liberal on social programs. But not always. It depended what they were."

Thus he was a centrist and a mediator. "I did try hard," he said, "to bring both groups together and I think that's proven by the fact that I had very good support from the legislature once we started to get the sewer project under control."

Then in the 1977 election, another seismic change occurred: 14 Republicans were elected as county legislators and 11 Democrats. Thus the Republicans had the majority, for the first time under the "new" county charter and under the legislature/county executive form of government. At the organizational meeting on January 1, 1978, James Mead nominated Gordon Anderson to be chair of the legislature, saying, "1978 can be the year when the Chautauqua county Legislature truly becomes an equal branch of County Government. To lead us into the future, it is my privilege today to nominate a veteran member of this Legislature . . . . Gordon Anderson has a reputation as being a peacemaker . . . .His wide experience on almost every committee of this legislature during the past six years uniquely qualifies him for this demanding and challenging position . . . .We need a person in that position who has a firm grasp of County Government, its policies and programs and its potential for a bright future. Such a person is Gordon E. Anderson of Ellery, and I proudly nominate him today for Chairman of the 1978 Chautauqua County Legislature."

Robert Barber was also nominated, but when the vote was tallied, Gordon was elected by 14 to 11. In his acceptance speech he echoed the wish of Mead and others for the legislature to be truly a cooperating bipartisanship, and he promised as one of his four wishes for the year that the committee chairs (now all majority members) would take pains to use the minority members fully and appoint them as chairs of subcommittees, because, he said, "I think it's important that everyone of us in this body are full participants."

He also expressed a hope that the legislature this year would "have better communication with the Executive." He said, "Our Charter has set up County Government into branches so we will have a separation of powers, and we will respect this, but we do not want the separation of powers to generate inefficiency and detachment and isolation."

But it was not to be the smooth sailing he hoped for. As Gordon had previously indicated, now that his party was in the majority and now that he was their elected leader, his responsibilities increased enormously. Both he and his caucus felt the need for more help, especially in the matters of parliamentary procedures and legal counsel. By law under the County Charter which had been accepted by county voters in 1975, all legal advice to the Legislature, the County Executive and all departments and offices of county government were to be provided by the County's Department of Law, under the authority of the County Attorney. But the County Attorney (Edwin Kuzdale) was a Democrat who served by appointment, under the charter, by the County Executive. The Legislature's new majority did not trust that legal advice from that source would be nonpartisan.

Therefore, early in 1978 they introduced, and passed with a 14 to 11 vote, a resolution to appoint their own parliamentarian and legal counsel, to serve approximately 30% of his time, at an annual salary of $8,000. The resolution was promptly vetoed by Executive Gerace on the grounds that it was a violation of the charter which clearly stated that "all legal resources of County government shall be centered in the Department of Law, which shall constitute a pool of legal talent, responsible for providing to the County Legislature . . . legal services and advice of any nature."

"[My colleagues] taunted me sometimes," says Gordon, "especially in my first term as chair when I didn't have an advisor unlike my predecessor, Frank Bratt, who of course was a Democrat and so drew on advice of the appointed Democratic county attorney. So a lot of the time I was left to my own interpreting of the rules and then the Democrats would say 'well, let's vote on that,' so sometimes my decision was sustained and once in a while it was not. And my own Republican side didn't always agree with me, and that was a hard part because it tied in with establishing our own identity as a Republican-controlled legislature.

"I think, too, that there were many things I didn't know from a legal point of view. However, I learned, quickly, a lot about county law because I had to. I did it by experience and by listening and by talking to other people and a lot of times I did talk to the county attorney because a lot of times it did involve the county and not just Republicans and Democrats."

The resolution of the problem of needing their own counsel was eventually resolved, but not without some highly publicized maneuvers which included Gerace's snipping apart the resolution and its amendment, which was Bill Parment's idea, and eventually, the legislators taking him to court over this and two other issues all in the name of "establishing our own identity as a Republican-controlled legislature" and working out the kinks in one branch of government (the legislature) and working smoothly with another (the executive). The full story of these maneuvers is told in the following chapter "A Tale of Two Men".

The first year of Gordon's legislature chairmanship was "critical," he said, "because of all the problems not just in trying to establish our identity, but also when I was faced with the letter that said that we were overdrawn many millions of dollars on the sewer."

In the conflict over that very serious problem, Gordon learned that his predecessor had left no documentation of his years as legislature chair. This created another problem, leading Gordon immediately to authorize setting up files for his record so that when he left the chairmanship he left copies of every document he had been responsible for or privy to.

As was stated in the previous chapter, Gordon was by state law, the one in charge of the sewer projects. In addition to all his other duties, therefore, he was the one where the buck stopped. And not only the buck, but when the financial crisis was revealed, the contractors working on the sewers threatened to shut down. Gordon describes this as his "darkest day." "No wonder I felt like Hans Brinker trying to prevent a disaster."

That "darkest day" was September 15, 1978—the day the overdrawn sewer spending was revealed. Gordon did not immediately inform anyone of the matter, realizing that he needed to learn, if possible, all the facts before rushing to judgment and leading the legislature to premature action. Almost two weeks later, Gordon was "severely criticized" (the *Post-Journal* said) "for not immediately making public the information that the authorized spending limit in the South Lake District had been exceeded by $3.5 million," and for proceeding with what the accuser, Roland Rapp of the Concerned Citizens of Chautauqua County, said "almost looks like a cover-up."

Gordon responded by saying he had asked County Attorney Edwin Kuzdale and full-time county employees to investigate when change orders on the contracts had been negotiated, resulting in the overspending. Meetings between the Concerned Citizens, the newly appointed Sewer Task Force, the new South and Center District executive director, Angelo Bennice, and others tried to find solutions to the financial impasse. Early in October, County Executive Gerace, Gordon Anderson, Mr. Bennice, and Sewer Attorney Gregory Yaw traveled to Albany to meet with the Environmental Facilities Corporation and the Urban Affairs Department of the Secretary of State's Office to seek a solution through issuing bonds to raise the needed money.

Ultimately the South and Center Sewer Districts' money problems were solved by the County's extraordinary action, through the legislature and the executive, of invoking "police powers" in order to keep the sewer construction from closing down. The action, in the words of County Attorney Kuzdale in his annual report for 1979, "was confirmed by acts of the State Legislature last May. This bold action. . . certainly resulted in savings that could be in the millions, since it became possible to continue the project at a time when it looked as though the contractors would quit, commence breach of contract actions for delay, require new bids which would undoubtedly have resulted in higher costs to the Districts."

Thus, Gordon recovered from his "darkest day," and the sewers were finally back on track to completion, as the story has been related in Chapter Eight.

However, the battles of those years of legislature chairmanship—January 1978 through December 1979—took their toll. Complying with his own wishes—to get back to his teaching, and other things he wanted to do—and with his family's concerns for relief from the constant hostility directed towards them all because of the sewer and landfill battles, Gordon announced his decision not to run for another term in the legislature.

He was not exactly "home free" yet, however; no sooner had he announced his intention to retire from public office than he was solicited once again—for the third time—to be his party's candidate for County Executive, running, of course, against the by then thrice re-elected Joseph Gerace.

When he was first solicited to run for County Executive, in preparation for the first election for that office (authorized by the newly adopted County Charter) to be held in 1974, one of his supporters wrote to him as follows: "I'm planting your qualifications on this basis: a new personality (not tired, shop-worn, selfish); a good brain; a hard worker; unshakable integrity—and a good, good intelligent campaign, with no name calling . . . . It's an honest assessment."

Thus, already, after his short two years in office, he had earned respect. He was asked again to run for the office in 1977, but again he declined (perhaps already aware that if he won re-election to his legislative seat he would be in line to be legislature chairman, should his party win the majority—which they did).

In 1981, however, when he was again sought to be the Republican candidate for County Executive, Gordon did not—nor would he have been able to—accept the nomination. He did not really want the race, and complications over what would have to be some sort of leave from his teaching, should he win, deterred him. He had already once before sought permission to take an extended leave of absence from his teaching at Jamestown Community College and had been denied. He knew the situation had not changed.

However, he did indicate that a change was in the offing. "It is my understanding," he wrote to his prospective nominators on January 12, 1981, "that a bill is in the state legislature which would extend the right to New York university professors to take leaves of absence for serving in elective office. This right would be extended to community college teachers also. But that is a long shot, and I have no other details just now.

"I have often dreamed of running for the office of Executive and feel that I have the administrative training and skills for the job; but, at this juncture, it doesn't look very hopeful for the reasons stated above. Therefore, I consider the matter closed as far as my candidacy is concerned."

As he and the man who had been his Majority Leader, James Mead, prepared to leave office, they were the subjects of newspaper interviews and analysis of what the two years of Republican majority in the legislature had accomplished. They both pointed to two major contributions: rather constant efforts to establish the integrity of the legislature and make it more independent of—and complementary to—the Executive branch; and tightening the reins on fiscal restraint. These translated into specific actions, sometimes resulting in controversy. Controversial ones were the effort to get their own legal counsel and resource assistants, a struggle over appointment of the public defender, and a budget impasse over the 1980 budget. Non-controversial achievements, involving cooperative efforts between the legislature, the executive, and others were the agricultural Center on Turner Road off Route 60, funding for the Dunkirk Small Boat Harbor Project, and important pre-action studies on issues in efforts to hold back spending.

2) Gordon Anderson and Legislator Dick Babbage reading the proclamation

As Gordon left the legislature, at the January 2, 1980 meeting, he was given a standing ovation for his two years of service as chair. As an article in the *Post-Journal* summarized his career: " . . . Anderson earned a reputation as a peacemaker among his colleagues. He commanded orderly meetings, was generous with time limits for speaking members of the public, and would supply a timely quip in tense moments."

He was feted with numerous tributes also at the "legislative banquet" that was one of the traditional events of winding down a term. Interestingly and appropriately enough, he was once again the subject of a special tribute[2,3] from the Chautauqua County Legislature in summer of 2003, twenty-five years later. That this biography was being written in the wake of such a reprise is testimony of why the story of those years, and of the career of Gordon Anderson is a story that should be told.

Dr. Gordon E. Anderson
Public Servant

WHEREAS, Dr. Gordon E. Anderson was born in Jamestown, NY and graduated from Jamestown High School, and

WHEREAS, Gordon returned to the area after college with a young family in 1963, to teach at his old alma mater, and

WHEREAS, After four years at Jamestown High School, he was hired to teach at Jamestown Community College, eventually becoming Professor of Psychology and Director of the Scandinavian Studies exchange program. He retired in 1994 because of ill health, and

WHEREAS, He has been very active in the Christian ministry for forty-nine years, and

WHEREAS, In 1972 he was elected to the first Chautauqua County Legislature, representing the Towns of Ellery and Gerry, and

WHEREAS, In 1973 he sent out the first County opinion poll to his legislative district which called for action on Chautauqua Lake pollution, and

WHEREAS, In 1976 he proposed a Chautauqua Lake management district to deal with the environmental problems of the lake, and

WHEREAS, In 1977 he called time and again for a full-time person to represent the County's interests in the construction of the South and Center sewer district, and

WHEREAS, In 1978 he was elected Chairman of the Legislature and called for an independent legal advisor and parliamentarian to the Legislature, and

WHEREAS, By 1978 the County's troubled South and Central sewer district was reeling out of control with a $7 million cost overrun, Gordon helped hold the project together and get it back on track, and

WHEREAS, His greatest achievement has been his firm hand and even temperament in guiding the County Legislature through some difficult time, therefore let it be

RESOLVED, That the Chautauqua County Legislature commends Dr. Gordon E. Anderson for his hard work, endurance and many accomplishments, and be it further

RESOLVED, That Gordon brings credit not only to himself, but also to his friends, his family, and all of Chautauqua County.

RICHARD BABBAGE, LEGISLATOR
District 17

KEITH AHLSTROM, CHAIRMAN
District 1

March 26, 2003

3) A tribute, 25 years later

121

DR. GORDON ANDERSON:
SOME LEGISLATIVE ACHIEVEMENTS

1965-66   Realignment of the Southern Tier Expressway (U.S. Route I-86) (Citizen action before being elected to the legislature.)

1972   Won four-way Primary and subsequently won election to the Chautauqua County Legislature

Helped negotiate a 25-member legislature, representing 12 districts (This was the first legislature, as different from the former County Board of Supervisors.)

Urged the public to go with an elected County Executive over an appointed County Manager. Participated in the ceremonies opening the Southern Tier Expressway from Falconer to Strunk Road.

1973   Launched the first county opinion poll, by surveying the members of his legislative district about specific county issues.

Called for action against lake pollution.

1974   Along with Arden Johnson, called for on/off ramps for the Expressway to be added near Shore Acres; they were put in the plans.

Saw that the oversight on part of DOT—to assign new route numbers to old Routes 17 & 17J—was corrected.

1975   A second survey of members of his district found 68% opposed to a bridge over Chautauqua Lake as part of Southern Tier Expressway.

Worked to solve runoff problems from expressway construction.

Publicly committed to sewers around the lake, completion of the Southern Tier Expressway and construction of a bridge across the lake.

1976   Proposed a Lake Maintenance District (was the first to formally do so), which subsequently died in committee.

Was instrumental in beginning to establish the separateness and integrity of the legislature vis-à-vis the County Executive.

1976-77   Did an extensive study of ferry rates and use of the ferry across the lake from Stow to Bemus Point.

Conducted an extensive study of nursing homes in Chautauqua County, and the need for more such facilities.

Had the privilege of cutting the ribbon to open the Strunk Road to Bemus Point section of the Southern Tier Expressway.

1977	Called time and again for hiring of an Executive Director for the South and Center Chautauqua Lake Sewer districts, to oversee the work of the Environmental Facilities Corporation.

1977   Called time and again for hiring of an Executive Director for the South and Center Chautauqua Lake Sewer districts, to oversee the work of the Environmental Facilities Corporation.

Urged saving of the old iron bridge built in 1883 on old Gerry-Levant Road when new bridge was built; with help of Bill Parment, director of Public Works, bridge was saved.

1978   Became the first Republican chairman of the Chautauqua County Legislature.

Fought location of the county landfill in the Town of Ellery (his district).

Called for a legal advisor to the legislature, independent of the County Attorney.

Continued to work for the integrity and autonomy of the legislature in its work with the County Executive.

Led the initiation of three friendly law suits against the County Executive, in order to carry out mandates of the Chautauqua County Charter.

Faced what he called the "worst moment in my life"—when he publicly announced that the Environmental Facilities Corporation (EFC) had overdrawn $3.5 to $7 million in construction of the lake sewers. (His predecessor had not held the required public hearings.)

A third survey of his legislative district showed a reversal of opinion on the Chautauqua Lake bridge: now 71% in favor of it.

Participated in the bridge groundbreaking with Governor Hugh Carey. The County Legislature, now backing Gordon Anderson 100%, passed the "Police Powers" resolution to get sewer construction back on track; the State Legislature subsequently "legitimized" the police powers decision.

By mutual consent, Anderson turned management of the South and Center Sewer Districts over to the County Executive.

Participated in the dedication of the new Agriculture Building along with other dignitaries, including U.S. Secretary of Agriculture Robert Berglund and County Executive Joseph Gerace.

1979   Innovative vacuum sewers and pumps were funded by Federal funds, and the sewers were on their way to completion.

CHAPTER TEN

A TALE OF TWO MEN

n Gordon Anderson's records of his four terms of office in the Chautauqua County legislature, there is a letter to him from Joseph Gerace, dated November 9, 1971, that says:

Dear Gordon:

Congratulations on your victory as a County Legislator! Although we are on opposite sides of the political fence, I know that we share a mutual concern for Chautauqua County and its future.

As you know, most of the pertinent issues which come before the Legislature are not of a partisan nature. It will be a pleasure to work with you. I will appreciate it if you will judge me not by reputation but by your own personal evaluation as we work together on county matters.

Again, congratulations and best of luck to you.

Very truly yours,

(Signed)   Joe Gerace

In some respects, this is one of the most interesting documents among all those consulted in writing this book. Although this is the story of Gordon Anderson's life, with particular attention to his service as a leader and model citizen as a governmental figure, a teacher, a minister, and a businessman, it would be an incomplete account if it did not include such details as those of the relationship between Gordon and Joseph Gerace, who were certainly leading protagonists (and sometimes antagonists) in the political development of Chautauqua County government between 1971 and 1979.

The Gerace letter is interesting for a variety of reasons. It brought up several questions. Why did Gerace write this letter at this time to a first-time winning politician? Possibly because he already knew (or expected) that he, a

Democrat, would be elected the first chairman of the Democrat-controlled (by a margin of 14 to 11) first Chautauqua County Legislature. Possibly, therefore, he sought to forestall disruptive internecine conflicts with the warm and conciliatory reminder in this letter that most of the matters that would come before the legislature would not be "of a partisan nature. "The hope that "you will judge me not by reputation but by your own personal evaluation as we work together" reinforces this interpretation—that Gerace expected to lead, as County government went forward in the 1970s.

When he was asked in an interview if he had written in this vein also to other people who were successful in the November 1971 election, Gerace answered that yes, he had. And that's important to know. Still, to Gordon Anderson, coming away from his first political win, the letter surely influenced a certain response and mind-set favorable to Joseph Gerace as they embarked on forming the new legislature together, along with the other 23 members.

Gerace had first been elected Supervisor of the Town of Busti in 1953, and thus had a seat on the County's Board of Supervisors. At that time he was 26 years old, and had, after serving in the U.S. Navy in 1945-46, earned both a bachelor's degree from Dennison University and a J.D. law degree from Albany Law School. Young as he was, he was nominated to be chair of the Board of Supervisors in 1961 and again in 1964, though in both cases the Republican nominee was elected by the Republican-dominated Board.

In the fall election of 1965, Gerace chose to run as the Democratic candidate for the seat in the New York State Assembly then held by Bruce Manley. Since he could not run for both the assembly seat and the one for town supervisor, he was then temporarily out of politics when he did not win the 1965 election. By 1969, however, he was once again on the ballot for the position of Busti town supervisor and won, so he was back on the board in 1970 and, from that year on until he resigned as County Executive in 1983 to take a position in State Government in Albany (as Agriculture and Marketing Commission, a cabinet position), he was probably the dominant Democrat in County government.

Although the Board of Supervisors had, in 1970, as it had had throughout the County's history, a Republican majority, Gerace tried hard to influence the future of the county by his attempt, early on in the year's business to get the Board to adjourn the organizational meeting to await the judge's decision on reapportionment. This was a decision resulting from a suit brought by Gerace and Dr. Glenn Ebersole to change the representation of the Board of Supervisors from having a number of representatives based on weighted voting—that is, one from a district having a greater population would have a weighted vote counting for more power than someone else coming from a less-populated district. Following the 1970 census, those who favored the suit wanted districts drawn on the basis of one-person, one-vote—i.e. each member of the board of supervisors' vote would count only as much as every other member's. Districts would still involve their population, in that a high-population district might have more than one member, but each member's vote would have equal weight, in the same way that each voter's vote in an election has equal weight.

Gerace's attempt to adjourn the 1970 organizational meeting failed, the meeting was held, and Republican Richard Evans was again elected chairman, though once again Gerace was also nominated.

Reapportionment continued to be an issue throughout 1970 and beyond. When Judge Gaughan's decision was announced early in 1970, requiring that the County Board of Supervisors go to a weighted-vote system temporarily while they prepared a permanent plan for reapportionment in Chautuauqua County, they complied. For a period from March 13, 1970 through December of 1971, the Board of Supervisors operated under the weighted vote plan.

When the board convened in early January 1972, they were, now, the first-ever Chautauqua County Legislature, and the weighted voting was gone. Moreover, for the first time in the history of Chautauqua County government, Democrats were in the majority. Not surprisingly, Joseph Gerace, who by now had had nearly 20 years of experience in county government, was elected chairman. And Gordon Anderson was among the neophyte legislators working with him.

Thus, when the legislature convened in January of 1972, and Gerace was elected chairman of the legislature which would have a Democratic majority for the next six years (three terms); and when Gordon Anderson ("me being me") began to exercise his style of representing his constituents (as an activist, a concerned responder to problems and issues, and a person determined to try to help find solutions), the stage was definitely set for a pretty constant interchange between the two men.

It began, as has already been chronicled, with the need to decide reapportionment issues. As members of a three- or four person committee which grappled with the mandate for one person-one vote representation and decided to go with a 25-member body, both Gerace and Anderson exerted considerable influence here early on. The apportionment question took, perhaps, far more time than it ought to have. The small committee worked on it, the legislature worked on it, a larger reapportionment committee chaired by Dr. Ebersole worked on it and reported back, a plan was submitted, as required, to Judge Gaughan by April 1 of 1972, and, though approved by the judge, was rejected by the people in a referendum in November 1972. In the end, the legislature continued with the 12-district, 25-member, one person-one vote legislature that had been planned by the first small committee and that is the way it has been ever since.

Already by April of 1972 the issue of solid waste disposal was in the forefront. Both federal and state environmental agencies were imposing—and requiring—action to deal with waste disposal, recycling and pollution. Rumors of a sanitary landfill being planned for Townline Road in the town of Ellery brought letters from citizens against it and testimony from citizens at legislature meetings opposing it. A team of engineers had been hired to prepare a study on waste disposal and Legislature Chairman Gerace announced plans to appoint a legislature-citizen committee to follow up on the study. Gordon chimed in by taking a survey of his constituents on this and several other questions, with the result that a significant majority (75%) of those who responded, both in Gerry and in Ellery, opposed a landfill on the proposed site. It would be several years before the landfill issue would be decided (it finally was opened on another Ellery site in 1980), but, throughout, both Anderson and Gerace were involved, Gerace as presiding executive, Anderson as committee member/investigator and as representative of the district where the landfill was sited.

In May of 1972, Gordon teamed up with Legislator Ted Smith to introduce a resolution empowering the legislature chairman to request a public meeting to inform county residents about the proposed bridge over Chautauqua Lake on the Southern Tier Expressway, and to ask the state Department of Transportation to conduct an in-depth study of alternate routes around the lake. By November they both felt that enough progress had been made on both these concerns that they sponsored another resolution, endorsing the completion of the Southern Tier Expressway (and by implication, construction of the bridge). This resolution was unanimously adopted, though Gordon had indicated that he wanted his remarks sent along with copies of the resolution to the designated parties (the DOT and the Commissioner of Highways of New York State) because he wanted specifics about the design of the bridge in order to preserve the aesthetics of the lake area.

Through 1973 and 1974 Gordon Anderson continued to represent his constituents as best he knew how, with continuing attention especially to the looming landfill decisions, the efforts to get the lake sewer projects moving forward, and to get completion of the expressway and the bridge. Gordon also worked during each term to try to get the ferry between Stow and Bemus Point taken care of. Through these years Joseph Gerace continued as legislature chairman and the interaction between the two men went smoothly on the whole, since Gordon was not necessarily in the forefront on controversial issues and consequently did not come into conflict with the legislature chairman.

Then in January of 1975, with the new Chautauqua County charter approved in the November 1974 election, Joseph Gerace became the first county executive and the legislature continued with a Democratic majority, with Frank Bratt as its chairman. Now the dynamics changed. Gerace as executive had his mandate, as outlined in the new charter, and also his own—

along with his legislative cohorts and his newly appointed staff—agenda, not only for the state of the county but also its future. The legislature, on the other hand, heretofore the single governing body of the county, now had to work on a balance of powers basis: certain things were still, as they had always been, assigned to the legislature's purview while others were now the province of the new executive. Yes, Gordon, and others, had long felt that the county would be better served by having an executive in charge of actual government management; however, as they worked to smooth out the "kinks," Gordon and others, including Gerace, sometimes ran into roadblocks.

Perhaps the first strong test of this came in 1976 when Executive Gerace encountered what he considered to be overstepping their bounds and duty limits by both Gordon and legislator Joseph Lepkowski. Lepkowski earned Gerace's displeasure by trying to dictate the process of running a medical clinic in his district (Clymer). Gordon's "transgression," in Gerace's eyes, was his proposal to establish a lake management district, which he initiated in spring of 1976 by calling meetings of state legislators representing Chautauqua County, county legislators, county department heads, the county executive and other concerned citizens. Gerace accused both Gordon and Lepkowski of trying "to administer and run county operations, department heads and/or employees," and he said (as quoted in the *Post-Journal* on April 19, 1976), "both of these gentlemen bypassed their respective legislative committees."

Within a few days the newspaper reported that Gordon and Gerace had "settled their differences," and that, henceforth, "the primary areas of policy and approach [on problems of lake management] will be the responsibility of the legislature's Environmental Affairs Committee."

Gordon characterized this dispute as being within the problem area of "trying to establish legislature integrity vs. that of the executive" —a problem that he and his fellow legislators continued to grapple with throughout Gordon's service in the legislature. Meanwhile, the Lepkowski-Gerace clinic dispute was not as easily solved, but eventually was handled by health commissioner Dr. Sidney Finkelstein.

The Lake Management question did not yet go away, however, as Gordon continued to lead the legislature efforts to work towards establishment of a Lake Management District, but now it was through a duly authorized subcommittee of the legislature. Moreover, throughout 1976, Gordon was besieged by complaints from members of his district about the need for dredging in Bemus Creek, the Bemus Canal, and in other streams and outlets flowing into and out of the lake. Part of the blockage problem was, residents thought, the result of construction on the Southern Tier Expressway and the bridge. Part of it was due to unusually heavy rainfall in 1975. Part of it was the natural erosion that had occurred for years at stream outlets. As lake studies and publications about the lake verified, many of the lake-border areas, including Bemus Point, and others, had formed in this way.

The immediate problem was the need for dredging to unclog the most severe deposits. Gordon and Executive Gerace conceived a plan whereby the county would contract with the state to do some of the dredging, using a "Mud Cat" rented from the state, and applying the money earned from the state for the work toward purchase of the Mud Cat. Negotiation for all of this went on for months, requiring much contact between Gerace and the responsible people in the state agencies involved. In the end, however, the project came to naught, as the state refused to accept responsibility for all of the clogging, and insisted that any dredging done at all by these state agencies would only be by separate contract after the construction was finished.

For Gordon, as representative of his constituency, problems over the aging ferry also took a great deal of his time during this period. Once again a large portion of any controversy was over money—in this case how much users should be charged as fares in order to keep the ferry operation solvent and to cover necessary repairs. In so many of these cases, the amounts being charged users were very small amounts and not likely to cause people to stop using the ferry, especially since there was still no bridge. Still, the ferry problem, like how to manage the lake and how to eliminate pollution of the lake, threatened to become a tempest rather than a little spot of rain, and Gordon, who was in the middle of all of it because of where he lived, could never get free of dealing with the issues.

The 1976 county budget, approved unanimously by the legislature in November 1975 after tough work to make it viable, proved to be a harbinger of struggles to come between the legislature and the executive. This budget had an interesting feature in that it included, on paper, a two million dollar surplus, which Gerace was then going to have to "find" as the year got underway. What had gone on so far in the 1970s, as the new county government system progressed, and as the county took over more and more responsibilities for services to its citizens, was a steady increase upwards, both in what was being done for citizens and in the cost of all those measures. So far it had been done pretty much without a noticeable raise in taxes.

By the end of 1975, however, it seemed obvious that, as costs rose—a steady progression, of course, since costs never seem to go downward—raises in taxes would be inevitable. At the same time Republicans in the legislature were coming to a determination to hold the line on taxes and to be more prudent in authorizing new programs and services. Moreover, decisions over what to do about solid waste were just down the road and already the costs of building sewers around the lake were mushrooming. Anyone looking into a crystal ball at the end of 1975 could have predicted trouble ahead.

In fact, after the unanimous budget approval in November 1975, preparing and adopting a budget for the county thereafter became more and more difficult, as the history of the next decades would show.

In 1977, Gordon became minority leader of the legislature, after James Mead announced his unwillingness to serve again in that post. At that point, as indicated earlier in Chapter Nine, Gordon was regarded by many as "the most powerful legislator" in the body.

As the legislature organized for the year, and after his "famous" George Orwell quote as he took office ("We are all equal, but some are more equal than others"), Gordon led off by asking for a bigger Republican role as the legislature began its work for the year. "Too often, in my view, the work has fallen on the same people," he said, and he wished that the Democratic majority would call on the minority members to take over some of the load.

However, the year very quickly bogged down in controversy as a new effort (the second) to locate the county's solid waste landfill in Ellery took off and as citizens of Gordon's district geared up to seriously oppose the location. Throughout, even until the citing of the landfill in Ellery was a fait accompli, Gordon opposed the project, both personally and as a representative of his constituency. The legislature Proceedings show him voting no on every resolution that had to do with the solid waste site in Ellery. Therefore, no one in his district could accuse him of "selling them out" on this issue. In the end, though, his vote had little effect because the Ellery landfill went ahead in spite of his opposition, and it finally opened for business in 1980, just after Gordon had left the legislature.

The records for 1977 show Gordon working with Executive Gerace in usual ways, as indicated by several letters in the record. Nonetheless, in preparation for the 1977 election, when Gordon would run once more, for his fourth and final term, the Post-Journal sent questionnaires to the opposing candidates for each seat, asking their views on several issues. In answer to the question, "What do you feel is the biggest problem facing the county, and how would you as a legislator help solve it?" Gordon wrote:

"The major problem facing the county is a lack of effective administration by the executive and legislature: 1. The legislature acts often under deadline pressure, without deliberation. 2. Too many political appointments of inexperienced or unqualified persons. Our research shows that two-thirds are Democratic appointments; one-third are Republicans. 3. No strong leadership in the agriculture center costs; the project seemed to drift upwards. 4. Poor highways. The basic maintenance has often been cut to sponsor more 'glittering' programs such as the Chautauqua Movement. 5. Little formal policy developed, such as landfill policy."

When the election was over, and the Republicans, for the first time in six years, had won the majority of the legislative seats, to make a count of 14 to 11, everyone had to stand back and reassess the situation.

Gordon's take was, "Certainly the new legislature is not going to be dominated by the executive. I think there are going to be more checks and balances, a new spirit of compromise."

As he prepared to take over as legislature chairman, Gordon predicted that there would be a "rocky" period during which the legislature and the executive would test the waters and, eventually, settle into working together. One of his priorities was committee reform—to get the committees to work efficiently in advance on the issues that they found on their dockets, rather than have the legislature fall back on working as a "committee of the whole." He also expected that facing up to highway repair and what to do about the landfill would be two early and important tasks. Finally, he hoped both party caucuses would focus on setting priorities in a way they had not previously done.

Gerace, for his part, said that his biggest regret at the outcome of the election was that, with all but one Democrat legislator elected from a city, there might be a tendency for a city-versus-county feeling to develop. "It's going to be a challenge to both the executive and the legislature to exercise statesmanship," he said.

He did not predict smooth sailing, but thought that, as the Republicans now took over the decision-making responsibility there might be clashes. He was right. As early as the organizational meeting on January 1, 1978, the new majority caused a ripple by designating Richard V. Slater as the county's public defender. This touched off a controversy that ran on for months and involved, first, Gerace's threat to veto the appointment because of "a high potential for conflict of interest" with an attorney who had worked in the prosecutor's office now being on the other side as public defender. The legislature countered that it was its right to appoint the county defender and the executive had no say in the matter, and then the executive claimed to have the right to veto any resolution passed by the legislature. Gerace moved to hold back Slater's salary, in his capacity to "hold responsibility for all county affairs and for the proper accounting of every taxpayer's dollar spent by county government."

Though the threatened Gerace veto did not materialize, the salary controversy did, and in the end Slater went to court to get redress and, with a decision in his favor, did finally get his salary released, but this did not happen until June of 1978.

The next fracas was over Gerace's attempt to reappoint 19 members of the fireboard without consultation with the legislature to assure a political balance on the board. "No one cares, including me, what its political balance is since fires are not political," said Gordon, "but we do care about various board and commission appointments that help develop policies ultimately involving taxpayers' dollars. A distribution of political viewpoints is highly desirable and will be expected."

He continued, with emphasis on a longtime bone of contention for the Republicans vis-à-vis the Democratic county executive: "I wish to say as bluntly and pointedly as I can . . .that the Chautauqua County Legislature will not

1) Part of the legislature in 1978. Left to Right. Jim Mead, Bill Evans, Gordon, Don Coe, Frank Bratt, Tony Raffa, Chester Tarnowski

serve as a rubber stamp for the county executive's appointments. There are 25 thinking individuals[1] on the legislature, duly elected by the people, who have the right and obligation to evaluate the executive's appointments based on pertinent information . . . . Since 24 percent of the legislature is new this year, adequate information on appointees is especially critical."

In March, at the regular legislature meeting, the Republicans, in passing a routine resolution appointing County Attorney Edwin Kuzdale as acting executive in Gerace's absence, voted in an amendment which appointed John Foster, an attorney, as "legislative counsel and parliamentarian" on a part-time basis, with funding of $6,200. Calling it "blackmail" of the county executive, the Democratic legislators walked out of the meeting, refusing to vote. The Republicans held sway, voting for the measure in a solid 14-member block.

This new controversy continued the Republican attempt to, as James Mead characterized it, "achieve its prime goal in establishing the legislature as a separate and equal branch of county government."

A week later, County Executive Gerace, at a press conference, staged a dramatic move of literally scissoring the resolution and its amendment in two and announcing that he was vetoing the amendment. In the meantime, Foster assumed his work as legislative counsel, but without pay, as the legislature prepared for its 30-day deadline on what to do with the veto.

By March 30, newspapers were reporting "GOP Threatens Gerace with Lawsuit," as the legislature chairman called a special session to vote on Gerace's ultimatum.

"There is no provision for using a pair of scissors to cut out a portion of a resolution with which he disagrees," Gordon said. He added that the matter must be clarified, even if it takes a decision by a court, because it casts doubt on the legality of Kuzdale as acting county executive.

"Under the present circumstances of a mutilated document which appoints him, his ability to sign contracts on behalf of the county could be challenged," Gordon said.

3) A humorous moment at the dedication

Gerace, in turn, defended his action on the grounds that, under the law, the legislature could not, as it had tried to do, join two such disparate actions (the appointment of the acting county executive and designating a new position as legislative counsel and parliamentarian) in one resolution; that, he said, was why he scissored the resolution. Moreover, he said he was "disappointed and disgusted" that the legislature was being called into special session "over a patronage job for a lawyer." There are more pressing issues to be dealt with, he said, such as sewer problems, industrial waste, solid waste, health care, transportation and taxes.

Gordon agreed and said he regretted these constitutional problems. "But I ask the people . . . to understand that we are trying to more sharply define legislative and executive duties in an effort to make the checks and balances more effective. In the long run, I believe the government will be the better for it."

As the year wore on, the attention of both the legislature (and especially its chairman, who was still legally in charge of the sewer projects) and the county executive—and of the people of the county—was diverted to the continuing problems with the sewers of the South and Center Lake Sewer districts. Then in June a court decision from state Supreme Court Justice John Doerr denying Gerace's right to veto the salary to be paid to the public defender turned the tide in the checks and balances dispute between the legislature and the executive. The judge's decision corroborated the legislature's right to make its appointments and set the salaries thereto.

In commenting on the decision, Gordon said that the legislature had "finally established its own integrity as a separate and equal branch of county government," a concern that had plagued him from the time he assumed his role as a county legislator. Thus, public defender Slater was finally able to draw his full salary, but the question of the legality and integrity of John Foster as legislative counsel and parliamentarian was still unsettled, and he was still not being paid for his work.

In midsummer of 1978, however, came a respite in the sort of constant tug of war between the legislature and the executive: The Agricultural Center[2] was opened and dedicated[3,4] at its site on airport land owned by the County. Though the authorization for and the building of the center had not been entirely without controversy, the end result was one of the star accomplishments of the county government enterprise in the 1970s. Both Gordon and Executive Gerace had been involved in the lead-up, as had, of course, Director of Public Works Parment. As Parment described the process, they had here a piece of land that had great potential for exploitation of the view and location. They managed to

5) Planting a tree at the Ag Center dedication

hire architects from both ends of the county (a good move)."Both Nelson Palmer and Carol Gaasch [from the north county] were good in design," Parment said. "And Julie Netzger from Jamestown/Lakewood was strong in design and Dick England was strong in details. And I think the combination proved to be a good collaboration." So the Agricultural Center—this place where several of the services to the rural nature of the county could be met—became one of those successes of the 1970s. Joseph Gerace, as County Executive, and Gordon Anderson, as chair of the legislature, were, of course, obligatory presences at the dedication. U.S. Secretary of Agriculture Robert Berglund was the keynote speaker. The day—in mid-July—was ripe for things like a tree planting, which Gerace and Anderson together took care of. At the luncheon of the day, Gordon (a Swede) and Berglund (a Swede) sat next to each other. Twenty-six years later Gordon remembers that they both drank from the same water glass that stood between their plates, in the often normal confusion of whose is whose.

A footnote to this occasion is that there was a sort of reprise in the summer of 2003, when the Agricultural Center celebrated its 25th anniversary, with, again, both Gordon Anderson and Joseph Gerace present. It was an occasion for them both—and others—to look back with nostalgic pleasure at the accomplishments of the 1970s in Chautauqua County, not altogether in a sic transit gloria frame of mind, what with the 25-year-old tree there, like a grown child, to remind them of the days of beginning.

But then again, as the year progressed, sewer problems pressed on. Yes, there was now an executive director of the sewer projects, Angelo Bennice, whose over watch helped to put things back on track. But then came Gordon Anderson's "blackest day," in September, when he learned that the sewer costs were overrun by $7 million, that breach of contracts with workers who couldn't be paid was pending, that unless something extraordinary was done and in a hurry, everything that had already been accomplished would be for naught. The workers were ready to walk off the job and the entire projects in both the south and center lake districts were in danger of collapse.

Sewer disaster stories appeared almost daily in the local papers and Gordon, who by law was in charge—as chairman of the legislature—and who, with both his full-time "day job" as professor at Jamestown Community College and his part-time job as legislator-sewer CEO, was already over-whelmed, faced the 24/7 challenge of how to solve the sewer problems. He was not alone, necessarily, but constituents were up in arms, local groups formed to protest the developments, especially the very active "Concerned Citizens of Chautauqua County," and were threatening lawsuits, and the con-tractors and their workers were breathing fire. Things were not good.

As time went on, the angry Concerned Citizens also threatened to oust the entire slate of county officials who, they felt, had abdicated their respon-sibilities to the electorate in their handling of the sewer crises. In December these Citizens authorized steps to remove from office six top county offi-cials—Gerace, Comptroller Sally McCluskey, County Attorney Edwin Kuzdale, Parment, Finance Director Lorren G. Caryl and Planning Director John Luensman—and all 25 members of the county legislature. Fortunately such a drastic happening did not take place.

As has been chronicled in Chapter Eight, the sewer problems were even-tually solved, and, once again, it was largely through a cooperative arrange-ment between Gordon Anderson and Joseph Gerace. They agreed to turn management of the sewer projects over to the full-time Executive, who had staff to help with the workload. And, as Public Works Director William Parment says in his preface, Gerace assigned Parment to take control of the project and "the project was subsequently brought to a successful comple-tion." Though those words seem to reflect completion of the sewers in the South and Center Lake Districts as "a piece of cake," it was definitely more than that by far, and all the participants—Parment, Gerace, Bennice, long-time sewer board chairman R.Theodore Smith, and, of course, finger-in-the-dike Gordon Anderson, could finally breathe normally when it was done.

The solution of the sewer crisis was one example of the way Gordon Anderson and Joseph Gerace worked together over the years from their "opposing" positions in government. Another example would be to look at what happened with executive vetoes of legislature resolutions over the years. When Gerace assumed the role as county executive in January of 1975, one of the things he took seriously was the interplay between the county legislature, which was empowered by the county charter to do such things as make local laws and adopt resolutions, commission studies and investigations, make appointments to temporary boards, and others, and the executive/administrator, who was empowered to approve all local laws and resolutions and to administer all county affairs. His was a full-time job, both by legal fiat and by the extent of the responsibility. In addition, Gerace was a trained lawyer who had practiced law before and during his service in the legislature before being elected county executive.

One reason, therefore, for certain executive vetoes over the years, was that Gerace, the lawyer, in consultation with the county attorney, saw possible legal entanglements in some of the resolution requirements, or saw that the resolutions were premature, needing further analysis and data, or posed the danger of setting precedents which could cause trouble down the road. The two executive vetoes in 1975, the five vetoes of 1976, and the ten vetoes of 1977 more or less fell into these kinds of categories. Moreover, through the end of 1977 there were no legislative overrides of any of these 17 vetoes.

Then, in January of 1978, the new Republican majority, with its announced agenda of "establishing the independence of the legislature" and of holding the line on taxation, presented a potential source of, if not conflict, at least strong and serious analysis and perhaps disagreement.

The story of the first three executive vetoes—aimed at the appointment of the Public Defender and at the "scissored" amendment to the appointment of County Attorney Kuzdale—has already been told. There were seven other vetoes during 1978. Five of them were on technical grounds similar to those of vetoes in earlier years. A sixth resolution—on leasing space in the Unigard Building in Jamestown for county offices—was vetoed as "premature" because of a need for further "space study." Though the veto came as a surprise to the legislature who thought the transaction was a "done deal," no attempt to override was made. Finally, the 10th veto was on line items in the proposed 1979 budget. The legislature voted to override on three of these and the rest carried. It should be noted that several times during 1978 and 1979, in giving the reasons for his vetoes, Gerace said that he had consulted with Gordon as legislature chairman and that they had come to an understanding as to the need for the veto. That was, however, not the case with the Unigard veto, which surprised Gordon as much as anyone, as his comments today still prove.

There were, again, ten executive vetoes of legislative resolutions in 1979, some of them acknowledged as having the executive and the legislative chair in agreement on the reasons for the veto. However, the newly "independent and equal" legislative branch succeeded in overriding vetoes three times. In two cases, the executive can be said to have lost the battles. One was a resolution asking the governor to restore the state aid formula, which was based on the state income tax; Gerace opposed this because he believed lowering the state income tax was a prior need for a state being starved by lost businesses and income. The other was an authorization to lower the time period for foreclosure on properties delinquent in taxes from four years to two; Gerace's opposition here was based on what he regarded as fair and compassionate for people who had been faithful taxpayers for years and had run into financial difficulty.

The final veto for 1979 involved disagreements over certain items in the 1980 county budget. First the legislature made changes in the proposed budget and Gerace responded with a veto over certain of those changes. In his remarks on the reasons for his vetoes, Gerace said, among other things: "One of the most important results of the objections is to establish a stable tax rate. It is hoped that rather than the hills and valleys of the budget experience of the past twenty years, that the County adopt as its policy a stabilized tax rate so that year to year the taxpayers can expect a uniform rate, one that does not get deep cuts in an election year and increases in an off-election year.

Thus, as 1979 and, as it happened, the period of Republican majority in the legislature, drew to a close, the next year's budget traveled a rocky road. First, at the regular meeting on November 9, the legislature overrode, once again, three items in Gerace's veto. All the other items, except two, carried. The two, exempted by a ruling of the chair, involved mistakes in the presentation of the accounts and no action was taken on them. Following the discussion and votes on these items, a resolution from the finance committee (without the committee's recommendation) to conditionally adopt the 1980 budget was defeated by a unanimous vote (with two absent). Finally, at the November 21 regular meeting, two more resolutions were submitted by the finance committee, again without recommendation. The first was to adopt the final budget and make appropriations for the conduct of county government for the next year. For reasons similar to those presented at the November 9th meeting, the legislators once again refused to adopt the budget. The vote this time was 8 yes, 13 no, and 4 absent. A companion resolution, however, to authorize the tax levy, which would finance the government for the coming year, was approved by a 19 to 2 vote. The net result of all this meant that, according to both the County Charter and the Administrative Code, a budget that failed adoption by the legislature still became the budget for the next year. So four months of hard work to overcome the disagreements and problems essentially went for naught.

For both Gordon Anderson, whose final acts in the legislature were to rule on the knotty questions as his colleagues debated the budget, and James Mead, the Majority Leader, these meetings and the final one on December 28 were their last. As he prepared to vote on the tax levy resolution, Mead gave this rueful summary of the state of county government's effectiveness:

"I too feel it's time to authorize the tax levy . . . [but] perhaps the next legislature in its infinite wisdom and experience should take a very serious look at the budget procedures because two out of the last three years now this legislature has not adopted a budget and that certainly does speak somewhat to the inadequacies of the procedures. Twice now this legislature has refused, and three years ago it was under the Democratic control so it has not just been a Republican situation. I would hope the next legislature could seriously take a look at the Charter provisions and see if they can't come up with some better procedures than what we have to operate under right now."

Chairman Anderson responded (say the Minutes): "I would agree with you 100%." Back in January 1979, as the legislature organized for business for the year, and as Joseph Gerace gave his State of the County address, there were reasons to look, as Gerace said, to prompted "reappraisals for all of us in the new year."

As he had done before, he referred to the temptation to conflict between "us"—the legislature and the executive. "The people are not interested in partisan differences," he said, "only in our ability to resolve the difficult issues before us. To that end, it is imperative that I allocate more time to meeting with legislators more frequently on a person to person basis, and this I will do."

Then, in a nod to the announcement recently made by Gordon that he had decided not to run again in November for his county legislature seat, Gerace added: "I've been very pleased to work with your Chairman, Gordon Anderson. He has been an outstanding individual and I would look with regret to his announced retirement from public life. He is a good and decent man."

According to Gordon, as quoted in a news article assessment early in 1979, the biggest issues in 1979 were to be "resolving the problems in the South and Center Chautauqua Lake Sewer Districts, getting the new county landfill site in the Town of Ellery into operation, and maintaining the tax stabilization plan initiated earlier this year." The first two issues were inherited, but the tax stabilization was seen as the major Republican contribution since they had become the legislature's majority. It continued to be a concern for the Republicans as 1979 wore on, and as the budget debate at the end of the year once again proved.

In response to Gordon's announcement that he would be retiring from politics when his current term was finished, the *Post-Journal*, in an editorial, said:

"The pressure on Anderson as legislature chairman has been considerable, particularly concerning problems in the South and Center sewer districts.

"Perhaps his greatest achievement, however, has been his firm hand and even temperament in guiding the county legislature through some difficult

6) Joseph Gerace congratulates Gordon at a special recognition by the legislature in March 2003 as Dick Babbage looks on

times following the change in political control of that lawmaking body . . . . Potentially explosive situations were defused largely though the mediating efforts of Anderson, who worked diligently with the county executive to smooth over the rough spots and help redirect attention to other pursuits that were more in the public's interests."

Once again, too, at one of the year's public celebratory functions where Gordon and Joseph Gerace were in attendance, Gerace took the opportunity to pay tribute to the finger-in-the-dike colleague with whom he had experienced so much of both the bad and the good of the 1970s decade in county government—the years of what Bill Parment had called "the revolution." Inside the program for the event, which he then gave to Gordon, Gerace wrote an extraordinary tribute:

Gordon—

Thank you for your inspiration. You truly are a great man—a good man—a decent man. You have truly been a friend. You have forgiven me 70 times 7. If any human being exemplifies the teachings of Jesus, you do. We'll miss you—until you come back again.

Your friend,

Joe

The tribute has the ring of truth, as many others than Gerace have corroborated over the years. It helps to explain why there is considerable reason to tell Gordon Anderson's story.

PHOTO GALLERY-10

2) Architectural drawing of Ag Center

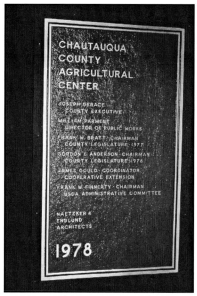

4) Bronze plaque on Ag Center building

PART 3

OTHER PATHWAYS

CHAPTER ELEVEN

A LIFETIME IN BUSINESS: SHOES, PHOTOS, AND OTHER "DELECTABLE THINGS"

hen Gordon Anderson first talked to the writer about doing a book about his life, he noted that the project appealed to him because he felt, as did others who knew him, that he had had such interesting, varied, and multi-faceted experiences. Look at all of it: He started out and continued in the ministry in some fashion all his life; early on, though, he veered into teaching, which he now describes as what he really loved best. Then he went into politics, where he had an eight-year career. Along with his teaching he did grant-supported research, helping his college to establish a psychology lab where he could get students involved in research as well. He initiated several significant enterprises, among them founding a community orchestra in his town and beginning and supporting a student exchange-study program between his college and the Södra Vätterbygdens Folkhögskola (SVF) in Jönköping, Sweden (begun in 1983 and continuing until 1996), thus furthering a connection between the Swedish community in Jamestown and their mother country.

Gordon had developed business acumen as a shoe salesman in Jamestown (in his teens, working for his uncles) and in California when he worked for the luxury-scale Joseph Magnin shoe store from 1954 to 1959. Visual literature (the comics, television, the movies) has milked shoe salesmanship as a joke to its limit. However, when it comes to sales savvy, no one, perhaps, is more exemplary than a successful shoe salesperson, which Gordon was.

Along with his wife, he was successful in several other business ventures. In California, early in their marriage while Gordon was waiting for a teaching job, for a time they managed the Trading Post in San Mateo. Here, people could trade in their old furniture, if it was in good condition, for new furniture. Often the "old" furniture that had been traded was genuine antique quality; consequently the Trading Post made more money selling the trade-ins than what the new pieces brought in. Moreover, since the Andersons were

1) North Shore Inn

newlyweds, the job was convenient because they were able to furnish their apartment at cost.

When they returned to Chautauqua County, business again became a focus. While Gordon was teaching at JCC, a well-known Chautauqua County citizen, Ed Cherry, asked him if he'd like to run a hotel and restaurant[1] at Chautauqua Institution for the summer of 1970. John Sellstrom and Robert S. Bargar had bought the North Shore Inn, planning to tear it down to build a condominium. However, Chautauquans wanted to see it run one more summer.

"After I talked it over with Geri," Gordon said, "I agreed to do it. I knew nothing about such things, but we were always looking for adventure. However, it really wasn't as wild as that. We leased the Inn for $1, and then we asked the former owners, Milly and Van Dyke Underwood, if they would live there at no cost in exchange for help and advice in running the 75-unit Inn. They agreed."

In addition to the 75 rooms, the Inn had a restaurant that seated 125. Besides feeding the hotel guests, the restaurant also was a popular spot for special dinners for groups such as the Swedish American Society and Alcoholics Anonymous. Over the summer the operation supported 35 employees. For the Andersons it was, Gordon says, "very interesting, profitable, and very long hours. It also sometimes had problems."

Once, on a Sunday, when facilities were crowded, the dock broke down[2] and people fell into the lake. Plumbing also usually chose Sundays to stop working when plumbers got double-time wages and the restaurant was full.

Because the Inn was part of Chautauqua, it spawned many interesting stories. For instance, Dr. John Voltman and his wife Jean met at the Inn when he was its first bellboy and she was a chambermaid. And the former owner, Van

Dyke Underwood had a lifetime license to pilot steamboats on Lake Chautauqua and, in earlier years, he took guests out at times. He was a good source of information on all 12 of the steamers, such as that the Golden Eagle[3] on top of one of the buildings had come from the pilot house of the lake steamer "City of Buffalo." It now hangs in a club in the Jamestown area.

3) The Golden Eagle from the steamer, "City of Buffalo"

During the summer of the Andersons' tenure, several famous people stayed at the Inn, among them Roberta Peters of the Metropolitan Opera and Dr. and Mrs. Ashley Montagu. Dr. Montagu showed himself to be a lovely, informal human being; to avoid the sometimes clamoring public, he enjoyed "dropping in" on his hosts for long chats. "Dr. Montagu," Gordon says, "was a lot of fun and he loved to tease both the hotel patrons and the waitresses."

Ms. Peters, as an opera star, did not like to eat before a performance. This caused the hotel managers to have to persuade their cooks to prepare a dinner for the lady late at night, after working their full day's schedule.Other guests in earlier years had included world-renowned pianist Van Cliburn and his parents and Big Band-era bandleader Artie Shaw.

There were seamier stories as well; for instance, one involving a college administrator/hotel guest who harassed and frightened the waitresses. (This is a story in and of itself.) Everyone was glad when he checked out.

And Gordon and Geri had a scare when their older son Dan, who was ten, was led off by a strange couple to an old diner on the other side of the Institution's fence. It was not clear what the couple's intentions were, but they did not seem to be good. The police directed the couple to leave the grounds permanently and, fortunately, they did.

Otherwise, though comparatively free for the summer to do what they pleased and mainly unsupervised, the boys (Dan, and his 6-year-old brother Dave) got along well. Once Dan caught some sunfish and asked the hotel cook, Alice, to fix them for his dinner. Dave, who had gotten up at 5:00 a.m. to go fishing, fell asleep over his dinner plate. In addition to Alice (Alice Merritt), there was one other cook, Virginia Champ, and a baker, Rufus MacIntosh. All three worked[4] at a sorority or fraternity house in the south during the winter and spent their summers at the North Shore Inn. "Very pleasant people, and good cooks," is Gordon's assessment of them. "The food was always very tasty."

All in all, as Gordon says, Chautauqua Institution and its parts, like the Nor   e. It made for an interesting summer. Yet, when the Andersons had a chance to run another hotel/restaurant the next year, they declined. "We, and our children," Gordon says, "needed to heal."

By 1973 Gordon was involved in his political career as a Chautauqua County Legislator. And by this time, Geri had gone back to school at JCC to take some courses, including some from Dr. Harry Bridges in his "Potential of Women" program. With his encouragement, she got the idea (which was planted by her husband) of starting a mail order business[5], called the North Shore Farmhouse, selling "Delectable Country Things" and working out of her home. Gordon came in as business partner. They started by marketing a water-saving device, selling to private homes as well as hotels and motels.

5) Catalog Cover, one of many drawn by Jane. E. Nelson

In an interview about the business in the trade journal Direct Marketing, in its March 1982 issue, Gordon is quoted as follows: "It [the device] was one of those things where once you sell an item like that, there is nowhere else to go with it. So we saw the necessity of having more than one item to sell, and since Geri is interested in crafts, we thought that might be an interesting thing to try. So she started to make up kits of what we call country flowers; they were made with calico and other fabrics. We advertised those, and that's how North Shore Farmhouse began."

6) The spice wreath, one of our most popular items

The centerpiece of their business was Geri's personally designed craft kits. Her flower kits and spice wreaths[6] became the most popular and she sold many thousands of them. Her forte was her ability to design the kits so that customers could use them easily and her clear and precise instructions enabled users to produce successful results. In the workroom of their "Carriage House" on Driftwood Road, Geri designed and executed many of the sale items. Gordon, meanwhile, devised marketing strategies. Together they wrote the advertising copy for the catalogs. Chautauqua artist Jane Nelson joined the operation by providing line drawings.

7) Presenting Direct Mail Marketing Association's Postmaster of the Year award to our own Postmaster, George E. Newman at Greenhurst

In ten years they built the business to include both crafts and craft kits, mainly designed by Geri, and "hard goods," such as kitchen equipment and other useful household and home-maintenance items. Their seasonal catalog mailings[7], several times a year, worked up to about 200,000. About 100,000 of those who received the catalogs were repeat customers.

Depending on the season, North Shore Farmhouse employed from six to twelve people and also along the way was able to use workers from the Association for the Mentally Retarded in Jamestown for packaging and other routine tasks. It also operated two catalog-outlet retail shops for a time, one locally and one in Virginia.

By 1985, Geri says, "We had expanded to the point of making a decision between a retail mail order business and the security which Gordon's position at the college offered. We opted for the security, considering the many years already invested in it, rather than the more precarious security of a retail catalog business. In that year we sold the entire business to a going concern of the same nature in Virginia. Ironically, we had helped the owners to form their business in earlier years."

8) Grand opening of Anderson Photo in Jamestown. L to r. Dan Anderson, Gordon, Dave Anderson, Mayor Steve Carlson

By this time, also, their sons David and Daniel had opened a retail photography supply shop[8] at 211 N. Main Street in downtown Jamestown. Their parents put up seed money for beginning the operation and to cover the huge costs for buying the photo processors.

The original conception for the store came from younger son David, who was attending Rochester Institute of Technology in pursuit of a bachelor's degree in biomedical photography. The timing coincided with the closing a month earlier of the former Johnson Camera at the same address. Some of the store's fixtures were purchased from the Johnson operation; several truckloads of fresh inventory were lent on a to-be-purchased basis from Richard Rowe, of Rowe Photo Video and TV in Rochester, NY, where David had been employed. This enabled the store to set up operations in a timely manner while establishing its own line of credit with the vendors. In keeping with the family-working-together motif, Geri worked at the store as a secretary.

The new business brought a different type of photographic service[9] to the area that Johnson Camera had not offered: One-Hour Processing[10]. In the fall of 1985, the Anderson sons purchased a second one-hour lab, and both locations offered photographic copying and restoration work, in addition to photo processing. By the end of the 1980s, Anderson Photo had three locations: 211 N. Main Street, Jamestown; 133 E. Fairmount Avenue, Lakewood; and at the Southside Plaza on Foote Avenue. In addition there were other drop-off locations throughout the area.

The 1990s, however, brought much development to the area (in part in the wake of the successful lake-sewering), and a new era of "mega-stores", all of which offered one-hour photo processing (including Wegman's, Wal-Mart, K-Mart, Eckerd Drugs, Quality Markets, and others). Moreover, many of the "cut-throat" discount chains sold cameras and photography accessories for less than what Anderson Photo paid for them directly from the factory. This led to the ultimate decision to cease Anderson Photo operations as of February 28, 1994.

12) A blanket of snow adorns the barn

During the nearly nine years in operation in the Jamestown area, many friends passed through the doors of the three Anderson locations. The photo business was truly a labor of love, given the stiff competition; it was very rewarding and a once-in-a-lifetime experience for the whole family.

As a sidebar activity to all of this family business enterprise, Gordon Anderson also pursued a lifetime of productive hobbies. He was a skilled woodworker and builder[11,12]. In his youth, he and his buddies used abandoned lumber to build a tree house. In spite of its success as a construction, the boys had to tear it down because of possible danger in using it. In later life, though, Gordon continued to indulge his hobby, building improvements to his house and property, building a barn for his horses[13,14] and helping his sons with their homes, and in other ways.

13a) Gordon's first horse

148

15) Gordon in Sweden on the farm of his Grandpa Louie at Ryggässen

Another of Gordon's interests is travel. He has not only crossed the United States 22 times, he has visited Sweden[15] eight times and on five of the trips his wife accompanied him. Other family members, sons, parents and brother[16] accompanied him at different times.

Also, Gordon and Geri have been to the Caribbean many times, visiting most of the islands. Their favorite spot is Antigua, where they have repeatedly stayed for two to three weeks. In 2001 they went to Tahiti[17] and in 2004 they went to the Panama Canal, which Gordon describes as one of the most complex engineering feats he has ever seen. It is so much more than the two little lines depicting it on a map.

Having grown up on Lake Chautauqua, Gordon naturally gravitates toward water. He and Geri particularly enjoy windjamming on the Schooner American Eagle[18] out of Rockland Harbor near Camden, Maine. One year they took a seven-day trip aboard the ship following the Eastern coast up almost to Nova Scotia.

Genealogy is another of Gordon's interests. Elisabeth Thorsell, a genealogist in Sweden, has helped him trace his ancestors there as far back as 1679. All were farmers except for one, F. E. Elmgren, who is mentioned in the beginning of this book.

PHOTO GALLERY-11

2) Waitress and chambermaids on dock at North Shore Inn

4) Part of the staff in the late 1960s Virginia Champ in back left, Rufus McIntosh extreme right center, leaning inward

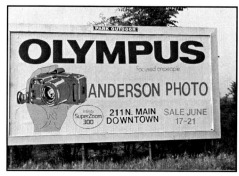

9) One of several billboards in the area advertising Anderson Photo

10) Workmen installing our one-hour lab

11) Framework for the new barn

13) Star pulling our 19th century buggy

14) Gordon with his horse, Teak

PHOTO GALLERY-11

16) Gordon, and his brother Dan, rowing a leaky boat on Lake Xyern at Grandpa Louie's farm

17) Over water bungalows in Bora Bora under a full moon

18) Our favorite schooner, American Eagle, out of Rockland Harbor, Maine

INTRODUCTION TO CHAPTER 12

By Eldon H. Johnson
Pastor Emeritus, Zion Covenant Church.
Jamestown, New York

1) Eldon H. Johnson

The motivation for "making a difference" comes from deep convictions, decisive decisions and serious discipline. In evangelical Christian circles, making a decision to accept Jesus Christ as Savior and Lord is often made at an early age at summer camps, special crusade meetings or through children's meetings at the local church. For many of us, decision – when taken seriously – becomes the dominant force in every area of life.

As a young boy, Gordon made this decision. Nurtured in a Christian home and encouraged in an evangelical church, he felt the call to Christian ministry during his junior high school years. With little encouragement, it was on to Chicago and North Park College and Seminary. Included in the seminary curriculum was a year of pastoral internship in a church, which, for him, happened to be in California. During this time, an opportunity in the field of education opened and a dual role emerged. God's call for him was not limited to one field.

Returning to Jamestown, Gordon continued the dual role. He reconnected with Zion Covenant Church where I was the pastor. We worked together on many different areas. As superintendent of the Sunday School, he decided on a contest to encourage our children to invite their friends. Following the command of Jesus to be "fishers of men," he offered little live gold fishes in plastic bags to anyone who brought a visitor, much to the consternation of parents of those children!

With Gordon as chairman of the church, we shared the joys and challenges of shaping the ministry of an older congregation in a new setting – i.e., a new building.

All along, Gordon continued to feel the call of God to pastoral ministry. As opportunities opened, he ministered in various churches for differing lengths of time; some for years – and varying distances – some demanding travel times of an hour or more each way, often in severe weather conditions of Western New York and Northwestern Pennsylvania.

Though his decision was made early in life, it impacted many people to make a difference in their spiritual lives and in many areas that have been expanded in the other chapters of this book.

I have appreciated Gordon's friendship, counsel and encouragement as I have attempted to "make a difference" in my own life and ministry.

CHAPTER TWELVE

THE CALL OF A LIFETIME: THE MINISTRY
by Gordon Anderson

B efore I begin this chapter, I would like to tell you this humorous incident, over which I have laughed each time it came to mind.

When the Spanish conquered what is now California, they built missions here and there, and also convents. One such mission and convent was built on Delores Street in San Francisco and was called Mission Delores. Keep in mind the name of this mission and the fact that I did my internship at the First Mission Covenant Church on Delores Street in the city.

2) Rev. Gerhard Palmgren

Now to the story: I offered to take the custodians of the church home after a meeting. I was driving my 1948 Plymouth through the labyrinth of streets in downtown San Francisco and accidentally went through a red light. A motorcycle officer pulled me over and stopped me. After a few questions he said, "Where do you work?" I told him "Mission Covenant Church on Delores Street." He replied, "S'cuse me Father, I never arrest anyone like you."

Thankfully, I rolled up the window and drove away as my passengers and I roared with laughter. I was only 21 years old. The story spread throughout the church like wildfire!

Many people do not know I served as a part-time pastor for nearly 50 years. Since it would be difficult for anyone else to write this part, I felt I should write it myself.

Serving as pastor of several churches has been a very rewarding experience in my life. To set the stage, let me first tell you about three pastors of Zion Mission Covenant Church in Jamestown who had a great influence on me as a boy.

Reverend Gerhard Palmgren[2] was the pastor during my early boyhood. He served the church from 1922 through 1938. He married my father and mother in 1931 and baptized me as an infant in 1933. He preached entirely in Swedish for the first four years of my life. It was hard as a little boy to sit still for an hour when everything was said in Swedish. Later the "revolution" came and it was decided to have one service a month in English. The transition was difficult, as I remember, but the church knew it had to make a change, even though it was hard on many people.

3) Rev. Nelson, my boyhood pastor

Pastor Palmgren accepted a call to another church in New York City and we called a new pastor, Reverend Gordon Nelson[3], who served the church from 1939 to 1945.

Pastor Nelson preached in English three Sundays out of four and in Swedish on the fourth Sunday to accommodate the older people, even though he wasn't as good in that language as the previous pastor had been. He baptized my brother, Daniel.

Pastor Nelson was a great organizer and during his pastorate the church celebrated its 50th Anniversary. Our country was at war in 1944 and he made a point of honoring Zion's servicemen and especially three who had perished.

To keep the Sunday School going during the war we went to Midway Park twice on the steamer, which was great fun. One year we went on the J W and NW trolley on the east side of the lake.

4) Rev. J. Theodore Johnson, the pastor who married us

In due time, Reverend Nelson resigned and took a church in San Francisco. An interesting note is that I did my internship out of seminary at the same church. However, Pastor Nelson was not serving the church at that time. Later, he would become the Superintendent of the California Conference and, as a result, I worked with him several times to get new churches started.

The third significant pastor in my life, Reverend J. Theodore Johnson[4], pastored Zion Covenant Church from 1945 to 1960. He came from Lindsborg, Kansas, and was extremely fluent in the Swedish language. This was, of course, pleasing to many of the older Swedes in the congregation. Pastor Johnson was a "pastor's pastor" and he knew the Word of God well. I grew, spiritually, under his ministry, for he truly was a man of God. He performed our wedding ceremony on July 26, 1958.

When my own ministry began, I am sure I used some of the techniques I had learned from the last two pastors.

5) Noble Chapel

Let me explain that I do not consider the ministry an occupation. For some it is only that, unfortunately. But I consider it a "calling" from God. Many people do not understand this concept, but I was humbled that God called me not by His voice but by events! What a thrill it was.

When I was just eight years old or so, I felt God's "call" to serve Him. I cannot rationally explain a "calling" but, as it developed, it was a feeling within. It was also doors opening and closing, such as going to North Park College and Theological Seminary; and God's people saying, "You are a good speaker for a young fellow," which further validated my call. As these things happened, in time, God showed me He wanted me to serve primarily as a teacher for earning my living and to also serve as a part-time pastor. By following God's leading I have had a wonderful and full life.

I had considered writing a brief history of each church I have served, but I decided the reader would be more interested in some of the events in my ministerial life. Some are almost funny and some are sad.

Before I do that, I think you should know that after my service at First Covenant Church in San Francisco, which is covered earlier in this book, I was somewhat disillusioned and for a time I didn't go to church. At that time I was going to San Francisco State University and also working as a salesman selling shoes and I "fell off the rails" for about two and a half years. At that time, a pastor of a small congregation that had been developed in South San Francisco would call asking me to come and play the violin for the service telling me that "if you don't, your fingers will get arthritic and stiff." Little by little I came back, for in my heart I knew what I was to do. Then this little church, which met at Noble Chapel in Cypress Lawn[5] Cemetery in Colma, California, developed a disagreement among its members and split. The pastor, who had been calling me from time to time, took a small number of the congregation to another chapel across the road in the cemetery. For a while, the small number went in one direction and we went in another. He had mailed out postcards telling folks the Sunday School had moved across the street. We prayed time and time again that if he and the small group were right that they would prosper. Otherwise we prayed we would prosper. It was determined by the Covenant Church that our group was the one that "abided by the constitution" that had been drawn up and we were allowed to continue using Noble Chapel in the cemetery as a meeting place and I became the volunteer part-time pastor.

Along the way, we acquired a large vacant lot on which to build a parsonage and a church building. During this period, Geri and I had met in Jamestown; she came to San Francisco at Christmas time and the next July 1958, we were married in the "old" Zion Covenant Church[6] in Jamestown, which stood next to Jamestown High School, where the high school swimming pool now stands. We returned to California as part of our honeymoon.

6) Old Zion Church

Geri became the 13th member of the church in South San Francisco and also my partner in ministry. She was the Sunday School Superintendent and taught Children's Church which we started and which was held in the crematorium. Because kids are kids, they would occasionally open the doors to the refrigerated compartments and say, "There is no one in here, nope, no one in here either, oh, there is one in here"! Of course, we had to put a stop to such nonsense.

About the same time, I met with the California Conference Superintendent, Gordon Nelson, who had been one of my boyhood pastors in Jamestown. I pled with him and the board to approve the start of a church building on the land we had purchased and which would be the only church in the middle of a housing development of 7000 homes, as I remember. It finally began, starting with a parsonage and later a church. We were able to call a full-time pastor who came shortly before we left the area and went to Arcata, which is about 300 miles north of San Francisco. I was hired for my first teaching position at Arcata High School. However, I still felt the need to be active in church work and we started a church there, renting a Seventh Day Adventist church, and built the congregation to around 40 or so who attended regularly. There simply were not enough committed people and the work was discontinued after two years. It is one thing to have those who attend but quite another if no one wants to do anything beyond that.

In 1963, God led us to leave California and return home to the Jamestown area. Without question, this was the hardest decision I have ever made and it came about after a series of complex events, feelings, answers to prayers and doors that opened while others closed. I had lived in California for ten years (even before the hippies did!) and never planned to return to Chautauqua County. But God knew what was best for us and for our developing family. Frankly, I was homesick for Chautauqua County and Chautauqua Lake. Lakes such as Chautauqua are sparse in California. While I was attending a school conference in Yosemite National Park, I was in a snowstorm for the first time in ten years. I was thrilled. I don't feel that way so much now, but it served to convince me that I really missed the seasons!

God blessed me with boundless energy in my life so that I was able to be a professor, a pastor and, for a time, a politician – taking my turn as I feel Americans should, if they are able.

The Bible is the most profound book ever written. God wrote it, for it could never have been invented. God used both Jewish and Gentile hands to write the Bible and I believe He has a plan for each person; He sure did for me. At the times when my footsteps went away from His perfect plan I got into mild trouble. He hadn't left me; I had left Him.

As a psychologist, I believe the human brain is the most complex thing in the known universe, and each of us has one! Both the Bible and psychologists say, "We become what we think about." If we think positively, we reap positive results; if we think negatively we reap negative results; if we think about nothing, we become nothing. The rule is, we reap what we sow. Seeking challenge in whatever we do helps our brain to maintain itself.

I've also learned that inner-directed people who live in harmony with God's plan for their lives are happier and more creative than outer-directed people who live only to please others.

Human behavior has not basically changed since the beginning of time. While we can boast about technological communicational advances, humans still cannot get along with each other. This is where God's forgiveness and grace, through Jesus' shed blood, is needed.

PREACHING

Serving as a pastor on a part-time basis was very rewarding, but was also difficult at times. The days are gone when a pastor had coffee with parishioners during a friendly home visit. Much of pastoring today is crisis counseling. Of course, sermons and Bible studies remain, but we live in troubled times and sometimes a lot of time is spent trying to counsel long after a devastating event such as divorce, which may have been avoided with proper counseling before it occurred.

Preaching is somewhat different from teaching. The hearers are volunteering their time in the former method. One time, as I was preaching my heart out, a mouse was seen running between the glass and the fluorescent lights in the ceiling. That was bad enough. I had lost the attention of the congregation. But a few weeks later, a snake was slithering around on the glass in the ceiling. All I could say was, "Satan is here today to hear the message." It was all lost, the snake won out.

Typically, I preach in an "expository" way, which is different from "topical". "Topical" is easier and some circumstances require a topical message because of the subject. Often, however, it becomes the speaker's opinion. "Expository" takes more skill and knowledge of the Scriptures, but in either case, I felt it most appropriate to present Jesus Christ as dying for our sin and rising again, as the Bible states. The Scriptures have always been my guide-book but, of course, I have failed many times and continue to do so, like most other humans.

BAPTISMS

The Evangelical Covenant Church and the Conservative Congregational Christian Conference have both ordained me. Both denominations allow either infant or adult baptism depending on how we interpret the Scriptures. I have sprinkled and immersed as people have requested. I have baptized several people in Chautauqua Lake as well as in immersion tanks or a baptismal font.

Infants and very small children are occasionally hard to handle for the sprinkling ceremony. Older children are easier. I had the privilege of baptizing our first grandson, Nicholas[7], and Nicolette[8], our first granddaughter. Our second granddaughter, Grace Elizabeth[9], who bears my initials, was dedicated instead of baptized, as was her sister Harmony[10]. Grace displayed her powerful lungs during the entire ceremony while Harmony slept through the whole thing.

WEDDINGS

Weddings are a time of great joy. But there are occasionally complications, such as pregnancy. The Bible teaches that the couple should get married first so the child will have a father and mother who are together and have made a public commitment to each other.

One wedding I performed was that of an elderly couple. She was a widow who was 84 and he was a widower who was 82. After they were married and established a home she found out that he had a girlfriend! The marriage was annulled.

Once I performed a marriage in the State of Pennsylvania. After the ceremony, I sat down to sign the license and found that it had been issued in the State of New York. So we raced over the state line and to a church where we redid the vows with my wife and the pastor of the church as witnesses, but without any wedding guests. This made everything legal.

Generally, I require three pre-marriage counseling sessions over a period of time. I did so with my own children, Daniel, who married Christine Harley, and David, who married Holly Cook. It was a wonderful experience to have had that privilege. For some reason, when I married David and Holly, and I said the vows to David, which I asked him to repeat, I said, "In joy and in sorrow; in sickness and in DEATH." Dave didn't know what to do so he repeated exactly what I said! I didn't realize I had made this mistake but the videotape is positive proof of my gaffe. My family teases me about it every once in a while.

FUNERALS

Unlike my colleague and classmate, who fell into the open grave as he performed a committal rite at a small rural country funeral, I have managed well. However, news of this unfortunate happening quickly spread throughout the denomination.

Funerals for close friends are very hard, but the hardest funeral I ever had was when my best friend at the college, Dr. John Collins, died suddenly at age 60. Mrs. Collins called in the early morning and said, "My husband died last night! Will you have the funeral"? Of course, I said, "Yes." Half of the college came to the funeral, including faculty, students and administration. Having survived serious complications after my own operation eight years earlier, I was able to share with them what God had done for me. But it was a very hard funeral as I was grieving over the loss of John along with the others who knew and loved him. After the service, Molly, John's widow, said to me, "John would have been proud of you." Those kind words made my day.

Another funeral for which I was asked to have the service was for a friend in Pennsylvania who died a slow death with colon cancer and who was a young man in his 30s. I was in the hospital room with him as he passed away and the heart monitor fell into a straight line. His family and I stood in a circle around him and held hands and prayed for each other, with thankfulness for his life. This man had accepted Christ as his Savior a few months before his death. We knew he had gone to be with his Creator and Redeemer.

Another funeral stands out in my mind. No one seemed sad except the mother of the deceased. He was a middle-aged man. Afterwards, his wife said to me, "I'm glad the old bat is gone." Even his children didn't show remorse.

I had a funeral for an 80-year-old man, who did not profess Christianity. He was sort of a grouchy fellow and I presumed it would be a very small funeral because of his advanced years. It was the largest funeral I had ever had! He had a very kind heart underneath his grouchiness. He was the kind of guy who would plow snow for people, pull them out of ditches and help whenever he could.

It's too bad the Bible doesn't say being good, helping people and doing nice things will save us. It does say that once we have accepted Jesus, then these nice things should follow as the result of our love for Him. Ephesians 2:8-9 says: "For it is by grace you have been saved, through faith – and this not from yourselves, it is the gift of God – not by works, so that no one can boast."

RECENT INTEREST

In the last 15 years I have become interested in Bible Prophecy and the Middle East[11]. I have studied it for perhaps 500+ hours. I am not an expert but I firmly believe we are in the end times according to prophecy. Three significant signs, which the Bible predicts, and are already fulfilled, are: Israel became a nation in 1948 (after 2500 years in exile!), Jews have been returning to Israel in great numbers (from 1950 to the present day), Jews own Jerusalem (1967, the six day war).

To me it seems very clear that the End is near when Jesus will return. Jesus said, "but as lightning comes from the east and flashes to the west so will be the coming of the Son of Man . . .Therefore keep watch because you do not know on what day your Lord will come." (Matthew 24:27 & 42)

I praise God for my ministry and for the souls who have found Christ as their Savior; for those who have been healed through prayer and/or Christian Counseling; for those whom I have married or baptized; and for God's call to the ministry. I have been richly blessed.

PHOTO GALLERY-12

7) Nick's baptism with his father Dan, Gordon and Uncle Dave

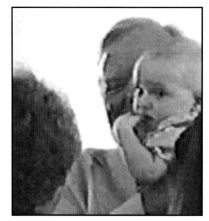

8) Gordon baptizes Nicolette

9) Gordon dedicating Gracie

10) Gordon dedicating Harmony at Zion's outdoor service

11) Announcing the Middle East and Bible Prophecy series

CHURCHES SERVED

DR. GORDON E. ANDERSON

San Francisco **First Covenant**	Youth Pastor	1953 – 1954	page 38
S. San Francisco **(later to become Grace Covenant)**	Pastor	1956 – early 1958	page 39
Arcata, California **Covenant**	Pastor	1960 – 1962	page 39
Eureka, California **Covenant**	Short Term Interim	few weeks in 1962	
Jamestown, NY **Zion Covenant Church** Sunday School Supt. (3 years) Chairman (8 years)	Layman	1963-1981	page 155
Bradford, PA **Covenant**	Pastor	1975 – 1980	page 162
Wiltsie, Russell, PA **Community Church**	Pastor	1981 – Oct. 1990	page 162
Kane, PA **Covenant**	Pastor	Nov. 1990 – May 1992	page 162
Ellington, NY **Congregational** later became CCCC	Pastor	1994-1999	page 162
Wiltsie, PA **Community Church**	Interim	Nov. 1999 – May 2000	

CHURCHES SERVED

1) Evangelical Covenant Church—Bradford, PA

2) Wiltsie Community Church—Russell, PA

3) Emmanuel Mission Church—Kane, PA

4) Ellington CCCC Church—Ellington, NY

EPILOGUE

Psalm 71:5-9

For you have been my hope, O Sovereign Lord,
my confidence since my youth.
From birth I have relied on you;
you brought me forth from my mother's womb.
I will ever praise you.
I have become like a portent to many,
but you are my strong refuge.
My mouth is filled with your praise,
declaring your splendor all day long.

Do not cast me away when I am old;
do not forsake me when my strength is gone.

CHAUTAUQUA LAKE MISCELLANY

Charts and illustrations courtesy of Thomas A. Erlandson and Linda V. Swanson, *Figure 8 the Lake*.

TABLE 34

List of Chautauqua Lake Fish Species[a]

Common name	Scientific name[b]
Paddlefish	*Polyodon spathula* Walbaum
Bowfin	*Amia calva* Linnaeus
Longnose gar	*Lepisosteus osseus* Linnaeus
Shortnose gar	*L. platostomus* Rafinesque
Spotted gar	*L. oculatus* Winchell
Common sucker	*Catostomus commersoni* Lacepede
Northern hog sucker	*Hypentelium nigricans* Le Sueur
Silver red horse	*Moxostoma anisurum* Rafinesque
Carp	*Cyprinus carpio* Linnaeus
Goldfish	*Carassius auratus* Linnaeus
Golden shiner	*Notemigonus crysoleucas* Mitchill
Redside dace	*Clinostomus elongatus* Kirtland
Creek chub	*Semotilus atromaculatus atromaculatus* Mitchill
Western blacknosed dace	*Rhinichthys atratulus meleagris* Agassiz
Mimic shiner	*Notropis volucellus volucellus* Cope
Blacknose minnow	*N. heterolepis* Eigenmann and Eigenmann
Blackchin minnow	*N. heterodon* Cope
Spottail shiner	*N. hudsonius hudsonius* Clinton
Western satin fin minnow	*N. spilopterous* Cope
Emerald shiner	*N. atherinoides* Rafinesque
Central common shiner	*N. cornutus crysecephalus* Rafinesque
Fathead minnow	*Pimephales promelas* Rafinesque
Bluntnose minnow	*Pimephales notatus* Rafinesque
Stoneroller minnow	*Campostoma anomalum* Rafinesque
Barred mad tom	*Noturus muirus* Jordan
Brown bullhead	*Ictalurus nebulosus nebulosus* Le Sueur
Black bullhead	*I. melas* Rafinesque
Mad tom	*Schilbeodes marginatus*
Muskellunge	*Esox masquinongy ohioensis* Kirtland
Grass pickerel	*E. americanus vermiculatus* Le Sueur
Banded killifish	*Fundulus diaphanus* Le Sueur
Brook silversides	*Labidesthes sicculus* Cope
White bass	*Morone chrysops* Rafinesque
Largemouth bass	*Micropterus salmoides* Lacepede
Smallmouth bass	*M. dolomieui* Lacepede
Bluegill	*Lepomis macrochirus* Rafinesque
Pumpkinseed	*L. gibbosus* Linnaeus
Rock bass	*Ambloplites rupestris* Rafinesque
Calico bass	*Pomoxis nigromaculatus* Le Sueur
White crappie	*P. annularis* Rafinesque
Western johnny darter	*Etheostoma nigrum nigrum* Rafinesque
Bluntnose darter	*E. chlorosomum* Hay
Rainbow darter	*E. caeruleum* Storer
Iowa darter	*E. exile* Girard
Striped fantail darter	*E. flabellare lineolatum* Agassiz
Log perch	*Percina caprodes* Rafinesque
Blackside darter	*P. maculata* Girard
Yellow perch	*Perca flavescens* Mitchill
Walleye	*Stizostedeon vitreum vitreum* Mitchill
Mottled sculpin	*Cottus bairdi* Girard
Brown trout	*Salmo trutta* Linnaeus
Rainbow trout	*S. gairdneri* Richardson
Brook trout	*Salvelinus fontinalis* Mitchill
Cisco	*Coregonus artedi huronicus* Koelz
Redfin sucker	*Moxostoma aureolum*

[a] Source: D. Bimber (unpublished).
[b] Nomenclature after Eddy (1969).

1) Fish Species found in Chautauqua Lake

CHAUTAUQUA LAKE
MISCELLANY

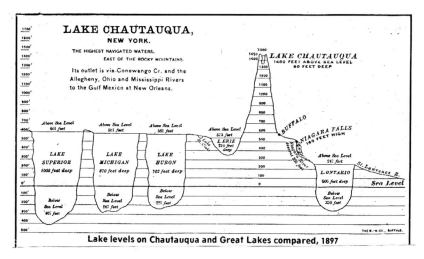

Lake levels on Chautauqua and Great Lakes compared, 1897

2) An 1897 comparison of the lake levels of Chautauqua Lake and the Great Lakes

3) Daughter-in-law, Holly Anderson standing on Whitney's Crib on December 13,1998 when the Lake was at the lowest level in recorded history, 1306.23 feet above sea level

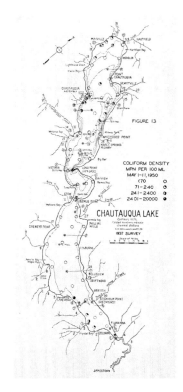

4) Chautauqua Lake from a 1937 survey

CHAUTAUQUA LAKE MISCELLANY

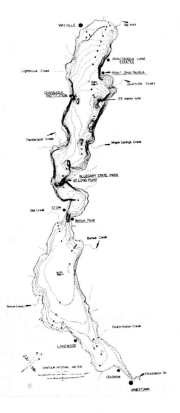

5) Bathymetric map of Chautauqua Lake in recent years

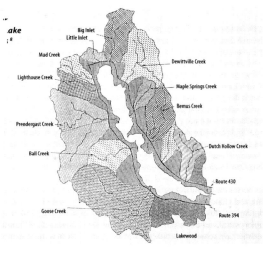

6) The major chautauqua Lake Watersheds

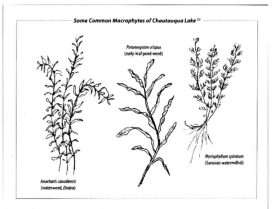

7) Some common Macrophytes of Chautauqua Lake

Chautauqua Lake Dimensions and Statistics [2]

	Northern Basin	Southern Basin
Length	9.20 mi. (14.8 km)	8.14 mi. (13.1 km)
Width, greatest	2.2 mi. (3.5 km)	2.0 mi. (3.2 km)
Width, mean	1.2 mi. (2.0 km)	1.2 mi. (1.9 km)
Depth, greatest	75 ft. (23 m)	20 ft. (6.0 m)
Depth, mean	26 ft. (7.8 m)	11 ft. (3.5 m)
Surface area	7071 acres (2856 ha)	6110 acres (2468 ha)
Volume	5.9 x 10^{10} gallons	2.3 x 10^{10} gallons
	(2.23 x 10^8 m^3)	(0.87 x 10^8 m^3)
Length of shoreline	10.2 mi. (16.4 km)	10.6 mi. (17.0 km)
Hydraulic retention	526 days	105 days
Latitude	N 42° 10'	
Longitude	W 79° 24'	
Drainage basin area	180.5 mi^2 (467.5 km^2)	
Elevation above sea level	1308 ft. (399 m)	

8) Physical description of Chautauqua Lake

CHURCH & OTHER INTERESTS

1) At the Welcome Booth at Mission Springs, the Covenant Camp in California, near Santa Cruz

2) A visit from my family taken at Muir Woods, CA 1954

3) Gordon skiing in the Sierras during Mission Springs Camp Season

4) Taking a break in Mission Springs

5) Gordon and his Youth Choir at First Covenant in San Francisco

6) Gordon as a new pastor in Wiltsie Community Church

7) Preaching at Wiltsie Community Church

8) Adding Sunday School rooms to the Wiltsie Church

CHURCH & OTHER INTERESTS

9) Pastor Gordon playing a violin solo at Christmas time in Bradford

10) Gordon and John Hallstrom, Chairman of the Bradford Church

11) Gordon serves as pastor of Family Camp II in 1988 at Mission Meadows in Dewitteville, NY

You are joyfully invited to be our guest(s) at a dinner celebrating the 50th anniversary of Grace Covenant Church, South San Francisco, and the symbolic burning of the church mortgage.

Sunday, September 19, 2004

Five o'clock in the evening

The Grosvenor Hotel 380 South Airport Boulevard South San Francisco, California

Special music by The Covenant Four

Please return the enclosed response card by Friday, September 3, 2004

12) The church that started in a cemetery in South San Francisco celebrates its 50th Anniversary

13) Legislator Anderson commemorating Handicap Awareness Week, May 13, 1979

14) Thom Shagla and Senator Jess Present watch as Gordon cuts the ribbon opening Route 17 Expressway in Aug 25, 1976

15) Breaking ground for a new bridge at Levant
Left to Right -
Assemblyman Dan Walsh, Legislator Paul Nelson, Chairman Gordon Anderson, Legislator Lance Spicer, Senator Jess Present, County executive Joseph Gerace(shovel), Mayor "Spec" Dye of falconer, Unknown, DPW Director Estabrook, Legislator Robert Kron, unknown

CHURCH & OTHER INTERESTS

16) The old Levant bridge is set aside to rest

17) Gordon in his office at JCC

18) Our first cruise to the Bahamas

19) Ready for a ride with horses and pony cart
L to R, Dave, Geri, Gordon, Dan

PHOTOS FROM THE PAST

1) The 1928 Buick my Grandpa Louie bought us so my Dad could drive him around

2) Ice harvesters on Chautauqua Lake

3) In years gone by, Jamestown's city sidewalks were plowed with horse-drawn plows

4) Bender's Pancakes stood on the site of what is now Vullos on Rt. 430

5) The old Fardink Sawmill on now Rt. 394. This was taken in the late 1800s. This is now the Ashville Bay Marina

6) Aerial view of the Fardink sawmill and home. The home still stands at the bottom of the hill on Rt. 394

PHOTOS FROM THE PAST

7) J. C. Jenkins Dairy in Lakewood in 1947. Roberts furniture and Jamestown mattress now occupy the site

8) A Jamestown Street Railway car made into a cabin at Phillips Mills c. 1940 (French's Cabin)

9) French's cabins at Phillips Mills. Six summer cabins made from Railway cars. Photo c. 1941

10) Chautauqua Lake Stock Farm est 1892 Photo C. Early 1900s Located on what is now Rt. 394 and Chautauqua Ave. in Lakewood

10a) Route 394 looking East toward Chautauqua Ave.

10b) Winch Rd looking North toward Rt. 394

11) An excursion on a steamer on Chautauqua Lake c. 1908

12) Pilot house of one of the steamers

13) I always felt the woman in this cartoon depicted my dear Mother

PHOTO CREDITS

Chapter One

#18 Connelly Park spring – Courtesy of Marian Marshall

#24 Houseboat – Courtesy Robert Johnston

#28 Trolley 100 picture – Courtesy of Robert Johnston

#43 Skating on the lake in Lakewood – Courtesy of Robert Johnston

Chapter Two

#2   Brostrom-Conner Shoe Store – Courtesy Richard Brostrom

Chapter Five

#10 County Court House, Mayville – Courtesy Donald L.Rexroad, Leisure Photography

#11 Legislative Office Building and Holland Land Company Vault – Courtesy Donald L. Rexroad, Leisure Photography

Chapter Six

#3   Cutting pilings – Courtesy Donald L. Rexroad, Leisure Photography

#4   Watson mansion – Courtesy of Robert Johnston

#5   Chautauqua Lake Bridge groundbreaking – Courtesy Rolland Kidder

#6,7 Ferry rates compared – Drawing by Jane E. Nelson

#8   Bridge, aerial view – Courtesy Donald L. Rexroad, Leisure Photography

#9   Bridge, aerial view – Courtesy Donald L. Rexroad, Leisure Photography

#10 Bridge, aerial view – Courtesy Donald L. Rexroad, Leisure Photography

#11 Bridge, aerial view – Courtesy Donald L. Rexroad, Leisure Photography

#12 Bridge Construction – Courtesy Donald L. Rexroad, Leisure Photography

#13 Bridge grid work – Courtesy Donald L. Rexroad, Leisure Photography

#14 Bridge, aerial view – Courtesy Donald L. Rexroad, Leisure Photography

#15 Bridge work – Courtesy Donald L. Rexroad, Leisure Photography

#16 Bridge, aerial view – Courtesy the Post Journal

#17 Bridge, aerial view – Courtesy Donald L. Rexroad, Leisure Photography

#18 View of Veteran's Memorial Bridge – Courtesy Linda V. Swanson, *Figure Eight The Lake*

#19 Long Point, aerial view – Courtesy Donald L. Rexroad, Leisure Photography

Chapter Seven

#1 – #4 Landfill excavation – Courtesy Chautauqua County Landfill, Sue Raines

Chapter Eight

#1 Sewer districts – Courtesy Linda V. Swanson and Thomas Erlandson, *Figure Eight The Lake*

#3 Celeron Sewer Plant – Courtesy Donald L. Rexroad, Leisure Photography

#4 Ground Breaking – Courtesy Ernest Leet

#5 Ground Breaking with JCC Professors – Courtesy Ernest Leet

#8 & #9 – Excavating for sewer at Center District – Courtesy Paul R. Johnson

Chapter Nine

#1 Floating algae – Courtesy Linda V. Swanson and Thomas Erlandson, *Figure Eight the Lake*

#3 Reading the Proclomation – Courtesy Chautauqua County Legislature – Photo by David Lelsz

Chapter Ten

#6 Congratulatory Handshake – Courtesy Chautauqua County Legislature – Photo by David Lelsz

Chapter Eleven

#2 Waitress and chambermaid on dock at North Shore Inn – Courtesy Burr Anderson.

#4 Cooks and staff at North Shore Inn – Courtesy Burr Anderson

Chapter Twelve

#1. Eldon H. Johnson – Courtesy Eldon Johnson

#4 J. Theodore Johnson – Courtesy Delores Carlson

Collage of Church related items:

#1 Bradford Covenant Church – Drawing by Jane E. Nelson

#2 Wiltsie Community Church – Drawing by Jane E. Nelson

#4 Ellington C.C.C.C. Church – Drawing by Jane E. Nelson

"Photos From The Past"

#3 Sidewalk Plow – Courtesy the late Roger C. Anderson

#5 Fardink Sawmill – Courtesy Mr. & Mrs. James A. Fardink, Ashville

#6 Aerial of Fardink Sawmill – Courtesy Mr. & Mrs. James A. Fardink, Ashville

#7 J. C. Jenkins Dairy – Courtesy Charles and Julianne (Jenkins) Peterson

#8 Jamestown Street/Railway Car – Courtesy Victor Norton. Harold Ahlstrom, photographer

#9 French's Cabins – Courtesy Victor Norton

#10,10a,10b Chautauqua Lake Stock Farm – Courtesy Lakewood Village, Joseph Johnson

Last Page of Book

#6 Family Photo – Courtesy Chautauqua County Legislature – Photo by David Lelsz

Note: All photos not listed are from the personal file of Gordon Anderson.

ABOUT THE AUTHOR

Joanne Schweik is a freelance writer and editor working in Fredonia, NY where she resides with her husband, Dr. Robert Schweik. As a writer she is the author of several locally related publications: among them are many articles and reviews published in such publications as *Artifacts,* the Dunkirk *Observer*, and the Jamestown *Post Journal*. She is the author of the long-running *Artful Kitchen* column, which ran in *Artifacts* from 1977 through 2003. She is also the author/compiler of *Chautauqua Cooks: A Century of Selected Recipes From Chautauqua County Kitchens*. More recently she has authored two histories of the terms of presidents of the State University College at Fredonia, *The Lanford Decade* and *The Beal Years*, both published by the Fredonia College Foundation.

She edited all three editions of Rolland Kidder's *A Hometown Went To War* (Real-life stories of World War II from Those Who Lived to Tell Them), which won a *Writer's Digest* Best Life Stories Award. Other editing assignments have included *Figure 8 The Lake: A Driving Tour of Chautauqua Lake*, by Thomas A. Erlandson and Linda V. Swanson, and *Telling Our Stories, 1883 –2000*, by Virginia C. Richardson (published by the Chautauqua County Historical Society).

INDEX

INDEX

INDEX

INDEX

INDEX

INDEX